VIRTUES AND VICES

CONTEMPORARY PHILOSOPHY

General Editor
Max Black, Cornell University

VIRTUES AND VICES

James D. Wallace

Cornell University Press

ITHACA AND LONDON

First published 1978 by Cornell University Press.
Published in the United Kingdom by Cornell University Press Ltd.,
2–4 Brook Street, London W1Y 1AA.

International Standard Book Number 0–8014–1142–4
Library of Congress Catalog Card Number 77–90912
Printed in the United States of America
Librarians: Library of Congress cataloging information appears on the last page of the book.

To Sally

Contents

Preface

My study of virtues and vices was begun in the hope of circum-
venting certain vexing problems in moral philosophy. I had
thought that if I concentrated upon character traits, the idea of
moral rules or laws could be dispensed with, and the familiar
problems about the origin, nature, and authority of such rules
avoided.[1] This proved to be a vain hope. Such virtues as honesty,
fairness, and being a person of one's word are indispensable elements in good character. These traits, which I call forms of
conscientiousness, are essentially attitudes toward moral requirements or rules. Not only are there problems about these
requirements, but there are related questions about what one's
attitude should be toward such requirements. Is it, for example,
altogether consistent with reasonableness and good judgment for
one conscientiously to keep one's word and to fulfill one's other
obligations, or is this conscientiousness a form of "rule worship"
and an abdication of one's moral and intellectual autonomy? If
one were sufficiently kind and compassionate, could one dis-
pense with conscientiousness altogether and still satisfy reason-

1. This program is suggested, if not exactly endorsed, by G. E. M.
Anscombe, "Modern Moral Philosophy," *Philosophy*, 33 (1958), 1-19.

able standards of human goodness? Certain traits, especially forms of conscientiousness, fit easily into a legalistic conception of ethics, whereas forms of benevolence such as kindness, compassion, and generosity are more easily accommodated to other views. My conclusion is that no conception of ethics can be satisfactory unless it has a place for both conscientiousness and benevolence. Both types of virtue are indispensable to us. A third type of virtue, represented by courage and restraint, is different in important ways from conscientiousness and benevolence. These traits have functions of their own, and a discussion of them raises still another set of issues.

The title of this book and the headings of its subdivisions sound old-fashioned. Virtue and vice are archaic terms, and courage, honesty, and generosity are no longer much written about—perhaps because they were once the subject of tiresome hortatory speech and writing. Traits of character, however, play an important part in our understanding of human behavior and in our evaluation of individuals and their actions. These ideas are rich and complex. They can be made to yield the most subtle and profound insights about human beings by wise and skilled novelists, historians, and playwrights. A philosophical study of character traits must deal with the most fundamental aspects of human life: value and evaluation—human goodness, merit, and responsibility; practical reason—action, desires, motives, reasons, reasoning, and judgment; and relations among people—community, convention, and shared ideals.

Human goodness—the goodness of a person—is conceived as a complex in which certain virtues or good character traits are functioning elements. Such traits reflect credit upon their possessors and tend to make them good people because the traits play various roles that are indispensable for good human life—for living well the sort of life that is characteristic of human beings. These various virtues, however, are connected with good human life in various ways. If an individual lacks certain of these virtues, then that person is incapacitated in crucial ways.

Preface

Other virtues, however, are such that although one who lacks them is not necessarily handicapped, you and I could not live well if most other people lacked these virtues. The nature and worth of all virtues can be understood by reference to the various functions or roles that they perform in our lives. Such explanations point the way to a conception of good human life that can be seen to be firmly grounded in the nature of things. This account is, broadly speaking, naturalistic, and certain key points are adapted from Aristotle.

Chapter II of this book is a slightly revised version of an article entitled "Excellences and Merit," which appeared in *The Philosophical Review*, 83 (1974). Incorporated in Chapter III is a revised and expanded version of a paper that appeared under the title "Cowardice and Courage" in the *American Philosophical Quarterly*, Monograph Number 7 (1973). I wish to thank the editors of these journals for permission to use this material.

I am very grateful to Wright Neely and to the University of Illinois for releasing me from administrative and teaching duties during the 1975–1976 academic year, thus enabling me to work full time on this project. The highly capable secretarial staff of my department has been a great help to me in preparing the manuscript.

Thanks are due to many students and colleagues from whose advice and criticism I have benefited, especially John M. Cooper, B. J. Diggs, Lester H. Hunt, Wright Neely, William N. Nelson, David S. Shwayder, Louis Werner, and Frederick L. Will.

When one's intellectual debts are sufficiently great, the desire to acknowledge those debts tends to conflict with the obligation not to implicate others in the shortcomings of one's own work. This poses for me an insoluble dilemma in the case of two colleagues. Their ideas have been of the greatest importance to me in this work. From B. J. Diggs, I have learned, among many other things, to appreciate the importance of community in morality.

Preface

The ideas of Frederick L. Will about knowledge, reasoning, and the philosophical enterprise have been for me not only illuminating but also profoundly stimulating and liberating.

I have the good fortune to be associated with an expert in the art of writing. Besides enduring a spouse's philosophical parturition, Sally F. Wallace has read all of the drafts of the manuscript and helped me in many ways to improve it. Readers of this book have reason to be grateful to her.

JAMES D. WALLACE

Urbana, Illinois

VIRTUES AND VICES

I

Goodness and Life

Particular virtues perform certain functions, play certain roles, in human life. A great number of factors in many different ways contribute systematically to human good, and virtues in specifiable ways so contribute as a part of such a system. Thus, an important function of such virtues as honesty, being a person of one's word, and truthfulness—virtues that are forms of conscientiousness—is to motivate individuals to conform to beneficial modes of behavior in certain sorts of situations. Such conformity, if it is sufficiently regular and widespread, makes possible activities and institutions that are necessary for communities and highly beneficial for the members of communities. Neither self-interest nor benevolence can, by themselves, fulfill this function as effectively as these forms of conscientiousness. Forms of benevolence, however, have functions of their own. Such virtues as kindness, compassion, and generosity tend to foster mutual feelings of good will among individuals in a community and to maintain individuals' sense of their own importance and worth. Such virtues as courage and restraint enable individuals to govern themselves, to pursue plans, to act on principles, and to participate fully in a life structured by intelligence, institutions, and conventions.

Virtues and Vices

The hypothesis that a virtue such as honesty or generosity has certain functions or roles can be useful in explaining certain otherwise puzzling features of the virtue, and it may afford an explanation of why the trait is a virtue. When the hypothesis that such and such a virtue has a specified function or role yields plausible explanations of both sorts, the hypothesis is supported.

In following this procedure, certain observations about human life are put forward to explain why certain traits of human beings are virtues, why the possession of these traits tends to make people good human beings, and why these traits make their actions good. It will be objected that to the extent that human life can be shown objectively to have certain features, these results alone will establish no conclusions about the goodness or badness, the rightness or wrongness of anything. They will, in other words, establish no *normative* conclusions. To the extent that a certain conception of human life does afford support for the claim that a certain character trait is important and valuable, then that conception will encapsulate certain normative assumptions. These normative assumptions, the objection continues, will not themselves be supported by the objectively established facts of the matter. The normative assumptions should be clearly separated from the facts, so that the objective status of the latter is not illegitimately transferred to the former.

It must be conceded at the outset that the conception of human life used in the following discussions is a normative one. This usage, however, is unavoidable, because life is a normative concept that cannot be understood apart from the conception of a creature's good. It does not follow from this, however, that dicta about a certain creature and its life divide into objective facts and subjective normative notions that exist in an epistemological vacuum. Among the facts about living creatures are how they live normally, under what conditions they flourish or languish, and what the proper functioning is of their parts. Knowledge of such things is indispensable for the biological sciences. It is the fruit of centuries of work by naturalists and physiologists. There is no reason in principle why a study of human excellences based upon the nature of human life need be any less objective, well founded, or authoritative than the study of any sort of living creature.

There is, of course, much philosophy to the contrary. Non-cognitivist theories of value take different forms, and the more influential versions are defended with ingenuity and tenacity by their adherents. Most arguments for these views, however, fall into one of two broad categories, although the two sorts of arguments are sometimes conjoined. The first type of argument employs the thesis that making a genuine value judgment involves the judger's being in some kind of affective state or his doing something—for example, his feeling a certain "sentiment,"[1] his "assenting to an imperative,"[2] or his "grading" things.[3] Feelings, imperatives, and grading activities are neither true nor false, thus they are not the sorts of things that might be objectively established as true or false. Insofar as these are somehow constituents or elements in value judgments, then such judgments cannot, in the last analysis, be established or shown to be true. These theses about value judgments are properly construed as accounts of the meaning of such judgments, and, as such, they are open to serious objections.[4]

Another type of argument for noncognitivism points to the seemingly endless controversies about certain sorts of value questions. It is alleged that an important difference can be seen between such disputes and actual disputes about matters of fact, a difference that indicates that fundamental disagreements about value questions cannot be resolved by purely rational means.[5]

1. David Hume, A Treatise of Human Nature, L. A. Selby-Bigge, ed. (Oxford: Oxford University Press, 1888), Book III, Part I, Section II, pp. 470–476.

2. R. M. Hare, The Language of Morals (Oxford: Oxford University Press, 1952) Part I, pp. 1–78.

3. J. O. Urmson, "On Grading," in A. Flew, ed., Logic and Language, 2d series (Oxford: Basil Blackwell, 1959), pp. 159–186.

4. See, for example, Peter Thomas Geach, "Ascriptivism," Philosophical Review, 69 (1960), 221–225, and H.-N. Castañeda, "Imperatives, Decisions, and 'Oughts,'" in H.-N. Castañeda and G. Nakhnikian, eds., Morality and the Language of Conduct (Detroit: Wayne State University Press, 1963), pp. 219–299.

5. See, for example, Joseph Margolis, Values and Conduct (New York: Oxford University Press, 1971), especially chapters 1, 6, 8, and 9.

The differences between controversies in morals and those in science, however, are much exaggerated.[6] Moral views do differ greatly from time to time and place to place, but this is equally true of scientific views. A modern physicist, an Eskimo, a fourteenth-century Franciscan, and an Illinois farmer would have as much difficulty agreeing about how the world is as they would about how it should be. Noncognitivists make much of the point that the relation between a value judgment and the factual grounds that can be given for it seems never to be logical entailment—as if it were common to find that our evidence for some important scientific view entailed that view.

In what follows, I will try to sketch a plausible alternative to noncognitivist accounts. I will defend a naturalistic view of human good, but one that has little to do with defining value terms or deducing evaluations from nonevaluative facts. Any study of living creatures as such, including modern biology, inevitably involves normative considerations. The view that life is a natural phenomenon leads to the conclusion that certain normative data are found in nature. Such normative data are properly studied by studying the lives of the appropriate organisms. On the basis of these considerations I will defend two theses. (1) It is possible to find in human life itself an objective basis for normative theses. (2) Certain facts about the nature of human life do yield explanations of why certain traits are virtues.

1. Normative Aspects of Biology

I have never been able to see why what is distinctive in the natural history of that species [i.e., *Homo Sapiens*] should appear—especially to a member of it—a less respectable subject of study than the natural history of the *paramecium* or the white rat.[7]

Let us now consider man in the free spirit of natural history, as though we were zoologists from another planet completing a catalogue of social species on Earth. In this macroscopic view, the humanities and social

6. See Alan Gewirth, "Positive 'Ethics' and Normative 'Science,'" *Philosophical Review*, 69 (1960), 311–330.

7. A. O. Lovejoy, *The Great Chain of Being* (New York: Harper & Row, 1960), pp. 22–23.

sciences shrink to specialized branches of biology; history, biography, and fiction are the research protocols of human ethology; and anthropology and sociology together constitute the sociobiology of a single primate species.[8]

Biology and social philosophy, including ethics, are alike in that a knowledge of what it is for certain kinds of creatures to live well, to flourish, is indispensable to both enterprises. Moreover, this knowledge is obtained and perfected by studying the kinds of creatures in question and the lives that they lead.

The training of philosophers is different in important ways from the training that prepares one to do research in modern biology. The two disciplines are different. I do not mean to deny this or to suggest that this should not be so. The idea that biology is similar to ethics and social philosophy is useful because it is of help in negotiating the hazardous epistemological waters surrounding the latter studies.

The sorts of lives that are characteristic of—and thus normal for—the many kinds of living creatures are by now so familiar that it takes a rather strenuous effort of imagination to appreciate what it would be like not to have such knowledge and what would be involved in trying to discover it for oneself. Biologists continually discover new kinds of organisms, but they know so much about living creatures that the new forms are invariably seen to be analogous to well-known creatures. Biologists look for novel sorts of environments or ecological niches to find new sorts of organisms. What they find are relatives of familiar forms specially adapted to the circumstances.

Whenever a novel type of ecological niche is explored by naturalists, a new fauna is discovered in it. The more aberrant the niche, the more extraordinary its fauna. The psammofauna of the interstitial spaces of sea-bottom sand, discovered by Remane, is a typical example. Who would have expected to find a jellyfish in such a habitat?! And yet this medusa (*Halammohydra*) has become completely adapted to this niche, which would at first sight appear to be totally unsuited for it. Any

8. E. O. Wilson, *Sociobiology: The New Synthesis* (Cambridge, Mass.: The Belknap Press of Harvard University Press, 1975), p. 547.

textbook of ecology will give further examples of such niches, like hot springs, alkalai flats, oil puddles, shifting sand dunes, and caves, that have been successfully colonized by organisms.[9]

Suppose, however, that one wished to study a truly exotic type of organism that is totally unfamiliar—a creature on Mars, perhaps. One must first discover what sort of life is characteristic of its kind. There is more than one way in which one might proceed, depending upon a number of considerations. One might simply observe a large number of creatures of this kind, noting what they do and what changes they undergo. This procedure could be very simple and straightforward, but serious difficulties might arise. It might not be obvious at first which are and which are not creatures of this kind. One individual may behave differently from another individual that looks quite similar. Are these two different sorts of organisms with different modes of life? Perhaps these individuals belong to the same species, but the differences in behavior are due to abnormalities or defects in one of the individuals. If so, however, which is normal and which is defective? It will be crucial too to form some idea of what circumstances are favorable and which are unfavorable for creatures of this kind. The mode of life that is characteristic of creatures of a given kind is the one that normal individuals of that kind will lead under favorable circumstances. These are all normative considerations.

Imagine a creature floating on the surface of a tank of sea water. Is it a normal, nondefective individual of its kind? If one knows that it is a fish of some kind, and it is floating belly-upward, scarcely moving, one has a basis for thinking that something is wrong. When all is well, fish do not behave in this way. Still, though, it may be a defective fish or it may be a healthy fresh-water fish that cannot live in salt water. If, on the other hand, the thing is a jellyfish, it may be behaving normally. The

9. Ernst Mayr, "The Emergence of Evolutionary Novelties," in *Evolution after Darwin*, Vol. I (*The Evolution of Life*), Sol Tax, ed. (Chicago: University of Chicago Press, 1960), p. 369.

notions of (1) the mode of life characteristic of an organism of a certain kind, (2) a normal, nondefective individual of the kind, and (3) circumstances favorable for that kind of creature are all interconnected. A knowledge of one will require some knowledge of the other two.

If one does not know about fish, however, it might be very difficult to work these things out for oneself. To discover what sort of life is characteristic of a certain kind of creature, one might observe a great many creatures of the same kind. How does one tell which are the same kind? This question aside, one cannot simply assume that the life characteristic of the kind is given by the way in which the majority live and die. In some species, most individuals never attain maturity. With all of these factors and complications, it is apparent that one would have to make several hypotheses simultaneously about the creatures, their mode of life, and the circumstances, and then observe the creatures and modify these hypotheses until one has a set of hypotheses that together make sense of what goes on.

It is obviously of enormous help in such an inquiry to have an extensive knowledge of many kinds of living creatures, their modes of life, the various structures of organisms whose functions adapt the creature to its mode of life, and the mechanisms of these structures. If one also understands how these forms of life evolved, and thus one knows which sorts of organisms are related and are apt to be similar to one another, this knowledge too can be useful in studying a newly discovered kind of creature. Biologists, who, of course, have this knowledge, bring it to bear upon new forms, looking for the analogies and relationships between new forms and other, well-known forms. Because the forms of life have been so extensively explored, classified, and fitted into well developed theories, new organisms, when they come to light, fit into these schema without a great deal of difficulty. The questions raised above about how one discerns the mode of life of a kind of organism, how one distinguishes normal from defective individuals and favorable from unfavorable circumstances for its life, are more easily answered by noting the new organism's similarities to other well-known forms. A biologist fits the organism into the existing theories, and these questions are answered, because they have already been answered about related organisms and similar ecological niches.

To see the importance for biology of questions about a creature's mode of life, a normal individual of its kind, and favorable circumstances for it, one needs to imagine circumstances in which such questions are problematic. These would be circumstances in which the questions are not answered for analogous forms, or circumstances in which the inquirer does not have this information. Perhaps biologists will encounter such problems in studying life on other planets. We can see the importance and difficulty of such questions, however, by considering how an intelligent biological ignoramus might on his own study sponges, mollusks, or sea cucumbers, working out their mode of life for himself.

These questions, which would be difficult to answer in such circumstances, are normative questions. Viewed in a certain way, such questions seem impossible to answer by straightforward, empirical investigations. The data with which the inquirer must deal include both defective and normal organisms and favorable and unfavorable circumstances for the organisms. Generalizations about the data as a whole will embrace the defective and unfavorable along with the normal and favorable, yet any selection of the the data prior to generalization in order to exclude the defective organisms will presuppose the very distinctions that the study is supposed to establish. The procedure appears hopelessly circular and question-begging.[10]

It is not plausible to think that in determining what members of a species are defective, a biologist's procedure is hopelessly circular and question-begging, that the distinction has no objective basis in fact. Clearly, a biologist does not merely look at all

10. Similar arguments are used to show that normative moral theories cannot be objectively established. See, for instance, Joseph Margolis, *Values and Conduct*, chap. 6.

the individuals he can find, note their similarities, and generalize. It is this very narrow construal of the investigatory resources available to him that makes the problem look insoluble. What a biologist does, however, is to fit this problem into a vast network of concepts, classifications, theory, and lore. The broader his knowledge and the better his theories, the easier this is apt to be. It is an indication of the breadth and depth of contemporary biology that this sort of thing rarely seems problematic.[11]

Normative questions about living creatures strike us as alien to modern life-sciences. The physical and chemical aspects of life have been the focus of attention in this century, as physiologists seek to understand the mechanisms of life, the operations of the parts of living creatures. No processes or occurrences are found in living creatures, it is said, that are not known to physical science. Physics and chemistry are, of course, the most prestigious of modern sciences. They are also the paradigms of *Wertfreiheit*.

I have no desire to defend vitalism or the "autonomy of biology," nor do I mean to criticize the directions taken by modern biological research. Rather, I point to features of this science that are so obvious and unproblematic that they are usually overlooked. Biologists study living things, and different kinds of living things lead different lives. Some understanding of the sort of life a creature leads is necessary for understanding the functioning of a creature's parts. For a part of an organism to have the sort of function that interests physiologists, the part must play some role in the organism's life. It must somehow benefit the organism or its progeny.[12] The idea of a living organism as a system with elements or parts with specific functions is simply another norma-

11. For a brief discussion of similar problems in moral theorizing see John Rawls, A *Theory of Justice* (Cambridge, Mass.: Harvard University Press, 1971), §9.
12. For recent discussions of the notion of a function, see Larry Wright, "Functions," *Philosophical Review*, 82 (1973), 139–168, and Christopher Boorse, "Wright on Functions," *Philosophical Review*, 85 (1976), 70–86.

tive facet of our concept of life. Proper functioning, normal individuals, and the capacities to live a life characteristic of a certain kind are obviously closely related notions.

Although the questions a contemporary biologist asks may not be normative questions, normative considerations of the sort we have discussed determine what questions are asked. An inquirer takes it for granted that a function of a certain organ is to store sugar. He may ask, what is the mechanism by which the organ performs this function? If the mechanism is electro-chemical, then the physiologist speaks the language of physics and chemistry. He is, however, studying how the organ stores sugar, rather than, say, its acoustical properties. The organism needs stored sugar, while the fact that this organ slightly muffles certain sounds does no one any good. That the focus of much investigation is upon mechanisms in this way tends to push normative considerations into the background. Such considerations, however, are governing what physio-chemical occurrences are being investigated.

The *fact*, of course, that certain parts of an organism are so structured that they perform such functions can in many cases, perhaps in all cases, be explained in terms of random variation and natural selection. The "genesis of adaptation," according to one biologist, is to be explained in the following way.

Natural selection arises from a reproductive competition among the individuals, and ultimately among the genes, in a Mendelian population. A gene is selected on one basis only, its average effectiveness in producing individuals able to maximize the gene's representation in future generations. The actual events in this process are endlessly complex, and the resulting adaptations exceedingly diverse, but the essential features are everywhere the same.[13]

I point here to the normative nature of what is thereby explained—the fact of adaptation.

13. George C. Williams, *Adaptation and Natural Selection* (Princeton, N.J.: Princeton University Press, 1966), p. 251.

Goodness and Life

The relevance of the normative aspect of the life-sciences to the study of virtues and human goodness lies in the epistemological lesson of the former. It is not at all tempting to suppose that the norms central to biology have their basis in the emotional responses or the personal preferences either of biologists or of the organisms they study. It does not seem plausible either to hold that biologists derive their knowledge of taxa, modes of life, adaptation, and so forth a priori from pure reason. They learn these things, rather, by studying the organisms in question and their lives, bringing to such studies what ingenuity and knowledge of the world they command.

It does not follow, of course, that a knowledge of human good can be obtained in analogous ways. General theses about the impossibility of objective studies of normative matters must be abandoned, however, and the question of the objective study of human good examined anew. Moreover, when one has an understanding of the mode of life characteristic of a certain creature, one has also a basis for understanding what it is for such a creature to flourish, to live well. It does not seem unreasonable, then, to expect that one can learn what it is for human beings to flourish, to live well, by studying human beings and human life. It does not follow deductively from the fact that biologists find norms in nature by studying the lives of living organisms that normative matters of interest in ethics and social philosophy are discovered in the study of human beings and human life. That such studies will shed light on questions of ethics and human values would have to be shown by the success of such studies.

2. Aristotle's Program

Aristotle's writings on ethics and politics are examples of this kind of study. In *De Anima*, he propounds the theory that *psuchē* (soul) is the "first *entelecheia* of a body capable of life"—that is, the *psuchē* of an organism is conceived as the capacities and tendencies it possesses to carry on the activities characteristic of

25

the mode of life of the creature's kind.[14] A defective creature of a certain kind will be one in which the exercise of these capacities and tendencies is somehow impaired. We can conceive of the creature's good as the unimpaired exercise of these capacities. Thus, an individual's living well or badly will be a matter of its relative success in carrying on these activities. To understand what success in these activities is, one must understand the activities. This modest conceptual framework provides Aristotle with a basis for discovering the nature of living well by studying the lives of creatures. This is the rationale for Aristotle's procedure in *Nicomachean Ethics*, I, 7, where he asserts that one can discover what living well and doing well are for human beings by discovering the *ergon* of man—the sort of activity which is most characteristic of mankind. Living well will consist in success at this, which will be activity of *psuchē* in accordance with the appropriate excellence(s).

Ethics for Aristotle is a practical subject. Its most important use is in politics, where it should be studied by those whose task is to order a community and conduct its business. The sort of community Aristotle had in mind, a *polis*, he conceived as an association of free (i.e. nonslave) individuals for the purpose of living together as well as possible. Obviously, then, it will be important for the rulers to know what it is for human beings to live well. Ethics, for Aristotle, is the study of good human life, and the point of the study is to aid us in ordering our lives, individually and collectively, so that we live as well as possible.

In an important way, the intellectual background of Aristotle's social thought was like our present situation. There was an extraordinary diversity of opinion about what constitutes living well.[15] This diversity of opinion, reflected in the very different ways in which people actually live, together with the often ir-

14. *De Anima*, Book II, chaps. 1–3. See also J. H. Randall, Jr., *Aristotle* (New York: Columbia University Press, 1960), chap. 4.

15. For a comprehensive discussion of the historical and philosophical aspects of political thought in ancient Greece, see George H. Sabine, *A History of Political Theory*, 3d ed. (New York: Holt, Rinehart, & Winston, 1961), Part I.

reconcilable disagreements to which these lead, lends credence to the subjective relativism which maintains that such disagreements are in principle irreconcilable by rational means, because what a good human life is is somehow not a matter of objective fact.

Plato's theory of the form of the good directly opposed such subjectivism. On this view, things get their natures from participation in eternal, unchanging forms, and thus many things may have in common the same nature through participation in the same form. All good things have something in common in virtue of which they are good—these participate in the form of the good. The existence of these forms and the participation of things in forms are objective facts. Knowledge of the forms, according to Plato, is to be attained after mathematical and logical training that will enable, at last, a few gifted individuals to grasp directly the nature of goodness itself. There is, on this view, such a thing as what a good life really is, but the knowledge of it is esoteric. The diversity of opinion about the good life is not to be taken to support relativism or skepticism, because only a few are competent to have opinions of their own on this subject.

There are difficulties in Plato's view that make it useless if one adopts Aristotle's view that political science is a practical study for those who rule and that a knowledge of what a good human life is is indispensable both for this science and for ruling. There are bound to be disagreements among the apparently enlightened. How is the ruler or a student of political science to deal with this? How does one determine whether *anyone*—oneself or another— really has this knowledge? On this topic, Plato's view can be classed as intuitionistic.

Aristotle's criticisms of Plato's theory of the good are impressive, and they point the way to a more promising account. Aristotle rejected the notion that good is "something universally present in all cases and single," and thus his attack on the notion of the good has ramifications far beyond Plato's particular view.[16]

16. Aristotle's criticisms of Plato on good are found in *Nicomachean Ethics*, I, 6.

White things such as snow and white lead all have in common something that constitutes their whiteness, but, Aristotle says, there is nothing *like this* that all good things have in common that constitutes their goodness. Things of the most diverse kind are good—God, reasons, traits of character, quantities, opportunities, and places, to list a few. Such diverse things cannot have something in common in the way that white things do. [17] Moreover, Aristotle argues, if good were one and the same thing in all cases, there would be one science of the good, one subject of study. But there are many sciences of good; a good opportunity in war is studied in strategy and a good opportunity in the treatment of disease is studied in medicine.

Aristotle's point might be put this way. The *knowledge* of goodness in one kind of thing is apt to be *different* from the *knowledge* of goodness in another sort of thing. This is to be contrasted with the knowledge of whiteness in different kinds of things. If a child is taught to recognize white in slips of paper, he is then expected, without further tuition, to recognize white in clouds, snow, chalk, and white lead. If he cannot in this way transfer what he learned with slips of paper to these other things, then he has not grasped what it was that was being shown him with the slips of paper. By contrast, when someone is able to recognize good tactics after studying strategy, we do not expect him on the basis of *this* knowledge to be able to recognize good courses of treatment for diseases, good architecture, or good gymnasts. That someone cannot transfer his knowledge of good tactics to other things in this way does not incline us to suppose that he did not really grasp the goodness of the tactics. It does seem right to say, then, that the knowledge of good in tactics is different from the knowledge of good in medical treatments. In the light of this, one can understand the thesis that good things do

17. This sentence and the two that precede it are an attempt to express briefly Aristotle's point in 1096a23–29. His argument actually employs premises that involve his accounts of categories and predication. For a discussion, see W. F. R. Hardie, *Aristotle's Ethical Theory* (Oxford: Oxford University Press, 1968), pp. 51–58.

not necessarily have some one thing in common in the way that white things do. The thesis, too, seems entirely warranted.

It may be objected, Aristotle recognized, that Platonists distinguish between things sought for their own sake and things sought for the sake of something else. The former are called good by reference to the form of the good, while the latter are called good because they preserve things good for their own sake or ward off evils. Aristotle lists plausible candidates for the status of things-good-in-themselves: intelligence, sight, and certain pleasures and honors. If one attempts to say in what the goodness of these things consists, he argues, the account in each case is different. Aristotle could have made his point here by using the example of the good, the well-being, of a living creature. The well-being of a tree deep in the jungle, of a sea-urchin, and of a coyote are not instrumental goods—they are not goods merely because they promote or sustain *other* goods. Yet in the sense already explained, the *knowledge* of the good of a tree, a sea-urchin, and a coyote are all *different*. The *accounts* of these goods will be different. Aristotle concludes: "The good, therefore, is not some common element answering to one Idea" (1096b25–26).[18]

With the rejection of the notion that all good things must have some character in common as do all white things, Aristotle rejected the key premise in a variety of arguments for such things as a transcendent form of the good, a nonnatural property of goodness, a special faculty for intuiting goodness, and a distinct sentiment evoked by the things we call good. We are well rid of such curiosities, I think, but we are faced again with the subjective relativism to which Plato's view was designed to provide an alternative.[19] Aristotle reviews the alternatives that remain after reject-

18. In quoting the *Nicomachean Ethics*, I use the translation of W. David Ross, in volume IX of *The Works of Aristotle Translated into English* (Oxford: Oxford University Press, 1915). All quotations from Aristotle are taken from this translation. Sometimes I replace an English word with the Greek original.

19. Indeed, Aristotle's arguments against the idea of the good are part of the arsenal of weapons of contemporary noncognitivism. See, for example, Hare, *The Language of Morals*, chap. 6, and Urmson, "On Grading." Modern noncognitivists are often anxious to show that they are not subjective relativists, but

ing the idea that good is "something universally present in all cases and single." "But what then do we mean by the good? It is surely not like the things that only chance to have the same name. Are goods one, then, by being derived from one good or by all contributing to one good, or are they rather one by analogy?" (1096b26–29).

Aristotle's remarks about being and health in *Metaphysics*, Γ, 2, suggest a way of illustrating the possibilities enumerated in this last question.

> There are many senses in which a thing may be said to 'be', but all that 'is' is related to one central point, one definite kind of thing, and is not said to 'be' by a mere ambiguity. Everything which is healthy is related to health, one thing in the sense that it preserves health, another in the sense that it produces it, another in the sense that it is a symptom of health, another because it is capable of it. [1003a32–b2]

Health, as a condition or state of an individual, consists in certain capacities for living normally. A person who is in this condition is called 'healthy.' A certain complexion is called 'healthy', meaning that it is a sign that its owner is healthy. In formal English, a diet or a climate which is conducive to health is called 'healthful', but it is very common to hear 'healthy' used in this way too. Perhaps we mean by 'healthy', 'capable of health,' when we say, "Living things, not stones, are healthy."

A healthy complexion and a healthy diet have in common no more than a relation to health. It is not even the same relation, since one is indicative of health and the other conducive to health. Health, as a condition of a living creature, consists in certain capacities, but the capacities that constitute the healthy condition of a cow are different from those that constitute the healthy condition of a tree. Yet the capacities that constitute bovine health are capacities of a certain sort of body to live normally the life of a cow and the capacities that constitute arboreal health are capacities to live normally the life of a tree. Thus, as arboreal health is to a tree, so bovine health is to a cow. Health,

---

the differences between their views and subjective relativism seem less important than the similarities.

of course, is a kind of good, and these appear to be just the relations that Aristotle had in mind as alternatives to the idea that
good is a quality like white, "something universally present in
all cases and single."

Of course, all good things *do* have something in common—
they are good. It is obvious, too, that this is not a pun. Health, a
form of good (roughly, the good physical condition of an organism), refers to certain capacities of an organism, and these will
be different capacities for different kinds of creatures. The
capacities are different because they are capacities for different
activities, different modes of life. Health in trees involves being
able to carry on photosynthesis; health in dogs involves the capacity to run around. These different activities are similar, however,
in that they are both important parts of the mode of life of each
kind of creature. Health is the same in all kinds of creatures, in
that it is invariably a certain sort of capacity for leading the mode
of life of the creature's kind. As one moves from one kind of
living creature to another, however, such things as life, living
well, health, and the creature's good are different. These things,
however, are all "one by analogy." The *knowledge* of health or
life for one kind of creature is different from the knowledge of
health or life for another. This is because the relevant capacities
and activities are different. Thus all living things or all healthy
things do not have something in common in the way that all
white things do. (Whether "properties," in the broadest
philosophical sense, are more apt to be like *white* or like *healthy*
and *living* is an interesting question that I shall not pursue.)

It is not surprising, then, that those who assume that all good
things *must* have something in common as all white things do, are
forced to postulate strange properties and mysterious faculties for
perceiving them. Others, whose sense of reality is offended by
such doctrines, are tempted, as Hume was, to "discover" affective
states that always accompany our judgments about goodness.
Hume's modern heirs hold that there are certain activities that
invariably accompany our judgments about goodness, so that
what is "universally present in all cases and single" is a certain
activity involving the thing judged to be good. The idea, though,

that biologists are necessarily grading or commending organisms, when they determine that the organisms' parts are functioning properly and that they are flourishing, is not very plausible.

In every case, to learn what health is for a certain kind of creature, one studies the creature and the life that it leads. Similarly, to learn what it is for a particular kind of creature to live well, to flourish, one must study the life of that kind of creature. The accounts one will give of these matters will differ from one sort of creature to the next, so that the knowledge obtained will in this sense be different. On the other hand, different kinds of living creatures are analogous to one another in a great many interesting and surprising ways.

One may know certain things about the life of one sort of creature and not know the corresponding facts about another kind of creature with which one is nonetheless familiar. For example, we are now accustomed to the idea that flowers are reproductive organs of plants, but this was not known until the late seventeenth century. The knowledge of life and good differs from creature to creature in that one may recognize features of these with one creature and yet not see them in another kind of creature. This is in contrast to the knowledge of colors. Yet life and goodness are analogous in different creatures, and one may by study of the creatures come to see the analogies. These analogies may dawn upon one. What a revelation it must have been for Nehemiah Grew when he realized that flowers are the sexual organs of plants![20] Biology is, in an important way, a study of analogies, but it is no less an objective (and enormously successful) study for that. What is learned in the study of one type of organism can be of great help in learning about another kind. What is studied is different but analogous.

3. Human Good

The way to discover what it is for a given kind of creature to live well is to study that creature and the life that it leads. If we

20. Charles Singer, A *History of Biology*, 3d rev. ed. (London and New York: Abelard-Schuman, 1959), pp. 159–161.

approach the question of good human life in this way, however, our difficulties at the outset are just the opposite of those encountered in the study of exotic and unusual forms of life. We already know an enormous amount about human beings and human life, and there is a bewildering collection of conflicting theories and theses about human life. The task before us is not to make new discoveries or to turn up new information, but to select from what is already known, to criticize existing theories, and to arrange what is left in a way that will enable us to understand the nature of human virtues and why they are valuable. In this, of course, our procedure will be different from that of a modern biologist.

There is a striking disanalogy between our conceptions of a plant's or a beast's flourishing and a human being's living well. This disanalogy makes it appear that the study of good human life must be in principle very different from the study of the others. Our notion of a human being living well is bound up with a multiplicity of complicated moral and social values. There is an obvious conventional aspect to these matters, and therefore conceptions of good human life have varied so from time to time and from community to community. Human health may be studied as one studies the health of other living creatures, but the idea of a human being's living well, in the full sense, is so bound up with conventional values, that its study must be very different from the study of other living things.

The conventional aspect of human life makes it different from the lives of any other organism, and conventions do vary from time to time and from place to place. Since such conventions condition views of human good, any such view is apt to be relative to the values of some community or other. Some theorists, holding that there is no objective basis for preferring one community's values to another's, infer that it is impossible objectively to establish the nature of good human life. Others, however, oppose what is natural to what is conventional in human life, rejecting the latter and basing their view of how a person should live upon the former. Thrasymachus in the *Republic* and Callicles in the *Gorgias* play cynical variations upon this theme.

It is obvious that living well, living fully, flourishing for a human being is different from living well for other kinds of creatures. The most striking difference between human life and all other kinds is that human life is characterized by activities that are possible only in a community with elaborate conventions. Language, knowledge (which is transmitted and therefore cumulative), commerce, arts, morality, and politics are some important areas of characteristically human activities. A variety of other complex cooperative activities are aimed at achieving shared goals, activities possible only in a community with conventions. The point I wish to stress is that living a life informed by convention is natural for human beings in much the way that perception, nutrition, growth, and reproduction are natural. The former, however, happens to be uniquely human. A human being who is incapable of taking part in activities that require conventions is defective in the same sense in which a dog that is incapable of perception or a plant that is incapable of nourishing itself is defective.

I am not saying that eccentrics and nonconformists are necessarily defective individuals of our kind. Such people are able to talk, to learn, and frequently to live with others in a community; this is a form of life that involves assuming many conventional roles and engaging in many activities that require conventions. I am using the term, 'conventional,' in a broad sense to include all of the things that philosophers have called institutions and practices. By conventional activities I understand all the activities that philosophers, influenced by Wittgenstein, have called "rule-following" behavior.

In studying human life, then, one is studying something that is naturally, characteristically, and distinctively conventional. Since the lives of other animals and plants do not have this conventional aspect, the study of human life, as such, will be different from the study of other forms. It is important to keep in mind, though, that although human life is very different from, say, the life of a rabbit or a seal, these in turn are very different from the lives of sponges or oak trees.

The conventional aspect of human life is a natural phenomenon. It is essential to *human* life. It is closely connected with the conceptions of the normal, the defective, the well, and the good in human life. They are as fit subjects for objective study by serious inquirers as any other natural phenomena. The fact is, though, that, with some exceptions, biologists do not concern themselves directly with the conventional aspects of human life.[21] They relegate such matters to less successful disciplines such as anthropology, psychology, and sociology. Language, knowledge, morality, and community are extremely complicated phenomena and are not very well understood. Modern inquirers are apt to come to the study of these matters with the assumption that their normative aspects must be purged or ignored for scientific purposes. Thus, the central ideas of human life are reduced to something else that seems better understood. These Procrustean operations are sometimes so radical that all that remains of the victim in the bed is a thin slice of the torso. It may be that some day we will have a new *De Anima* that will embrace all forms of life. Perhaps then we will hear no more of the mind-body problem. The present lack of understanding of the conventional aspects of human life is not an argument that these matters are unfit for objective study.

Some of the variations in conventions and institutions from community to community will make little difference in the quality of life in these communities—whether, for example, the language of the community is Chinese, Arabic, or French. Other variations will make an enormous difference—whether the vendetta is the custom, for example.

Many conventions will have both advantages and disadvantages. According to Herodotus, as Xerxes marched his armies to conquer Greece, he asked a Spartan exile, Demaratus, how the Greeks, outnumbered a thousand to one and free to do exactly as they pleased, could hope to stand up to the Persians. Demaratus spoke, with some trepidation, of his own countrymen, the Spartans:

---

21. For one exception see E. O. Wilson, *Sociobiology*, chap. 27.

'Fighting singly, they are as good as any, but fighting together they are the best soldiers in the world. They are free—yes—but not entirely free; for they have a master, and that master is Law, which they fear much more than your subjects fear you. Whatever this master commands, they do; and his command never varies: it is never to retreat in battle, however great the odds, but always to stand firm, and to conquer or die. If, my lord, you think that what I have said is nonsense—very well; I am willing henceforward to hold my tongue. This time I spoke because you forced me to speak. In any case, I pray that all may turn out as you desire.'

Xerxes burst out laughing at Demaratus' answer, and good humouredly let him go.[22]

Some conventions will be essential for there to be any communities at all. Certain conventions will be better than others for a given community in a certain situation. Some conventions that greatly enhance life in one community may be destructive in another community. Some communities will be better than others. The important point, however, is that what is distinctive about human life is this conventional aspect. Whatever variations this form of life admits of, such things as *human* health, intelligence, conscientiousness, benevolence, restraint, and courage tend in their ways to foster it.

4. *Human Excellences and the Human* Ergon

I wish to focus attention upon the *form* of certain of Aristotle's accounts in his ethical and political writings, while to a considerable extent ignoring the content of these accounts. He provides us with general concepts and theses that link together human life, good, and excellences. (1) It belongs to the nature of some kinds of things that they do a certain "work" (*ergon*); for example, an eye *sees*, a carpenter *makes things of wood*. (2) A good one of such a kind is one that does its work well; a good eye is one that sees well, etc. (3) An excellence of a thing is a condition of the thing that "makes the work of that thing be done well."[23]

Aristotle held that human beings have an *ergon*, a characteris-

22. *The Histories*, Aubrey de Sélincourt, trans. (Harmondsworth, Middlesex: Penguin Books, 1972), p. 477.
23. See particularly *Nicomachean Ethics*, I, 7, and II, 6.

tic "work." This, he said, is activity of the part of us "having *logos*"—the rational part of us, as this is commonly translated (1098a2–8). Human excellences will be states or conditions of persons that make their activity good "work." Such activity—the human *ergon* done well—over a whole life he identified with *eudaimonia* (happiness, blessedness).

The account of *eudaimonia* in the *Nicomachean Ethics*, Book X, is implausible to modern readers, and it is based upon suppositions that we do not find compelling. Aristotle does not explain sufficiently the crucial notions of *logos* and activity *meta logou* (activity in accordance with *logos*). His sketch of the relationships among the other concepts, however, is highly suggestive. The examples of the eye and the carpenter can serve as very simple models to illustrate the relationship of the *ergon* of a ϕ (what a ϕ does that makes it a [nondefective] ϕ), a ϕ doing its *ergon* well, the excellences of a ϕ, and a good ϕ. Applying this model to human beings, human excellences will be tendencies and capacities for living well the sort of life that is characteristic of human beings. I propose to characterize the human *ergon* as a social life informed by convention, rather than activity in accordance with *logos*.

"A life structured by convention" is a simple description of something that is extraordinarily complex. It will not be easy to say briefly what living this sort of life consists in. Some of this work, however, is undertaken in the discussions that follow of particular virtues and vices. This very general characterization is necessary, however, in order to see useful analogies between these studies of human virtues and other familiar, unproblematic matters. Human excellences, including virtues, will be capacities or tendencies that suit an indivudual for human life *generally*. These traits are such that if they were lacking altogether in a group of people, these people would be incapable of living the life characteristic of human beings.

These virtues may be contrasted with excellences that suit an individual for just one specific kind of activity. Woodworking skill, for example, is a virtue of carpenters. Together with other qualities, this excellence would tend to make a carpenter a good carpenter. An individual with all of these qualities, who lived amidst the sort of material and institutional circumstances necessary for the craft, and who was healthy and fortunate in other ways, could have a successful career as a carpenter. One can grasp what it is to do well at a specific kind of activity, such as woodworking, by understanding the point (or points) of the activity and appreciating the problems and difficulties encountered by its practitioners. One can at the same time see what qualities of a carpenter would contribute to his doing well at his craft.

The notion of a human *ergon* provides a basis for a similar study of human life and human good. We study a creature that naturally lives a certain kind of social life structured by conventions. Regularly, we find language, politics, inquiry, commerce, and arts among other things. Human beings have certain physical and psychological characteristics, which determine certain needs and interests. Finally, these creatures live in a certain kind of world. In the course of living the sort of life that they naturally lead, they regularly encounter certain kinds of problems. By studying this sort of life, by noting the various purposes and goals of activities that make up human life and the problems encountered in realizing these purposes, we can come to understand what it is for a human being to live well and what characteristics of a human being contribute to living well. In putting the matter so briefly and simply, I do not mean to minimize the extraordinary complexity of this task. Of course, one may at the same time approach the matter from the opposite direction. On the assumption that certain virtues are human excellences, what must human life and human good be like? I propose to proceed in both ways.

This view of the matter and the analogy between a good person and a good craftsman is suggested by Aristotle in *Nicomachean Ethics* (I, 7). "Just as for a flute player, a sculptor, or any artist, and in general, for all things that have an *ergon* or activity, the good and the 'well' is thought to reside in the *ergon*, so would it seem to be for man, if he has an *ergon*" (1097b25–27).

II

Excellences and Merit

1. Action-States

The term 'excellence' will be used in this discussion much as Aristotle used the Greek word *aretē*. So, for example, both skills and good character traits are excellences. Unless otherwise indicated, the term 'virtue' will be reserved for good traits of character—such things as Aristotle's *aretai ēthikai*. I will use the terms 'action' and 'to act' to refer to anything that a person might be said to be able to do. Thus, such things as seeing, understanding, and enjoying are actions.

States of persons that are (or that involve as a major component) capacities or tendencies to act form a large and heterogeneous family. These I will call action-states. Each of these states is what Aristotle called a "first actuality," the further actualization of which is an act.[1] The following examples indicate the heterogeneous

1. Aristotle said that "actuality" has two senses that correspond respectively to the possession of knowledge and to the exercise of that knowledge. Learning that moss tends to grow on the north side of trees can be thought of as the realization of a certain capacity to learn, the actualization of a potentiality. Possessing the knowledge is a "first actuality," which is from time to time further actualized when one *uses* the knowledge, for example, to find one's way. At other times, the knowledge is dormant. The further actualization of this first actuality is "second actuality." See *De Anima* 412a22–27.

collection of states I have in mind: intelligence, sight, wanting to be a playwright, dishonesty, being in love, understanding a theory, fondness for sailing, physical strength, depression, musical talent, courage, and health.

Action-states form a family because they are substantially capacities or tendencies to act. It is obvious, however, that they are a motley lot, exhibiting considerable diversity. A comprehensive list of action-states might be rearranged into subgroups on a variety of principles of classification, and the various groupings would be different depending upon the principles used. Some of those states fall into natural and familiar groups under such headings as moods, skills, sentiments, character traits, and abilities. Although action-states have a fundamental unity—they are first actualities the further actualization of which is an act—the division between tendencies and capacities is important and basic. Skills are capacities to do things proficiently, strength is the capacity to exert physical force, sight the capacity to see, human health the capacity connected with the proper functioning of the human organism to do a wide variety of things that people normally can do. A fondness for sailing, however, is not the capacity to sail; rather it is a tendency to sail, to think about sailing. Moods such as depression and elation and virtues such as kindness and generosity are pretty clearly tendencies rather than capacities. Some action-states, however, show characteristics of both capacities and tendencies. Patience, for example, seems to be both the capacity to wait when waiting is difficult and the tendency not to be hasty.

The distinction between tendencies and capacities, often blurred in discussions of "dispositional properties," is of importance for the study of excellences. I will assume, however, that those notions and the differences between them are sufficiently clear for present purposes.

2. Excellences

In discussing moral and intellectual character, Aristotle employs the notion of an excellence (*aretē*). This suggests still another way of dividing action-states. Judging from the way Aristotle uses the term, human excellences form a subset of action-states, which includes good character traits, certain skills, and other states that have affinities both to good character traits and to skills (*phronēsis* (practical wisdom), for example). This subset cuts across the distinction between tendencies and capacities, having some members that are fairly clear examples of tendencies, members that are examples of capacities, and members having features of both. Human excellences turn out to be action-states that have a particular relation to good, meritorious, and praiseworthy performances and actions, and which at the same time reflect credit upon the agent himself. The states are bound up conceptually both with good actions and good agents. Aristotle makes this point in the following passage.

Every excellence both brings into good condition the thing of which it is the excellence and makes the work of that thing be done well; e.g. the excellence of the eye makes both the eye and its work good; for it is by the excellence of the eye that we see well. . . . The excellence of man also will be the state of character [*hexis*] which makes a man good and which makes him do his own work well. [*Nicomachean Ethics*, II, 6, 1106a15–23][2]

The example of the eye provides a neat model for Aristotle's view of the relationships to one another of (1) an excellence of a thing of kind *k*, (2) its being a *k*, (3) the thing's doing its "work" well, and (4) the thing's being a good *k*. If this model is somehow applicable to human beings and human life, as Aristotle thought, then *human* excellences—that is, excellences that make an individual a good human being—will be found to be action-states that are tendencies or capacities to act in ways that constitute living well as a human being—to do well the sorts of things that are characteristic of human life.

This concept of an excellence, however, selects from among action-states those that have a special connection with good or

2. In this particular passage, I have taken the liberty of changing Ross's translation so that *aretē* is always translated by "excellence."

praiseworthy action. It is clearly good to have sight, health, and strength, but the exercises of those capacities are not necessarily good performances or good actions. When an action is an exercise of skill, however, when it exhibits skill, then necessarily it is done well by a standard appropriate to the kind of action it is and the sort of skill in question. The traits that go to make up good character—the virtues—are also connected with good, praiseworthy, meritorious action. If an action is fully characteristic of a virtue, such as kindness, honesty, or courage, then there is something good to be said for the action and for the agent.

3. *Acts Fully Characteristic of Excellences*

The notion of an action's being fully characteristic of an excellence is a crucial one for this discussion. A particular action might be the sort of action that a certain excellence is the capacity or tendency to perform, and in this case the action is *characteristic* of the excellence. Not every action that is characteristic of an excellence, however, is also *fully* characteristic of it. To be *fully characteristic* of an excellence, an action must be *strictly speaking* the sort of action that the excellence is the tendency or capacity to perform. For example, an individual shoots an arrow that lodges in the center of a target one hundred yards away. Such an action is characteristic of skill at archery. Suppose, however, that the individual was not trying to hit the target. She was merely trying the bow, not intending to release the arrow, and she was not even aware that there was a target in front of her. The fact, then, that this individual shot an arrow that hit the center of the target, given this other information, has no tendency whatever to support the hypothesis that this individual is skilled at archery. Such an action would not be said to exhibit the skill. Her action, although it is characteristic of such skill, is not fully characteristic of it.

The important feature of an excellence is that an act *fully characteristic* of it will be good—well done—and it will reflect credit upon the agent. A central question for understanding the nature of personal merit (and demerit) is: what *more* is required to make actions that are *merely* characteristic of a certain excellence into actions that are *fully* characteristic of the excellence? Answers to this question are fundamental for an account of the conditions for the appropriateness of praise, blame, reward, and punishment and for an account of the derivative notion of responsibility.[3] Excellences are sufficiently diverse, however, that we must expect different answers to this question for different kinds of excellences.

If an action is fully characteristic of a virtue, then the action will be in that respect good, because of what a virtue is. Of course, one may still ask whether acting courageously, kindly, or honestly is acting well. To raise this question, however, is to raise the question of whether kindness, honesty, and courage are virtues. In this chapter, I will simply assume that they are virtues.

A disanalogy between virtues and skills becomes apparent when one attempts to ask an analogous question about a skill. There seems to be no question that skill at debating is a skill and that the acts exhibiting this skill are instances of good debating and debating well. Some skills are not worth having, however, and they are no less skills for that. On the other hand, we do not call a character trait a virtue—that is a good character trait—unless we think it is worth having. Even though we agree that a certain skill is not worth having, an action that exhibits the skill will be an action done well and it will reflect credit upon the agent as a doer of that sort of thing. A hypothesis that would explain this difference is that the virtues are human excellences, whereas these skills are not. The question whether a person is to be a debater arises from time to time, and thus the question whether it is worth having the necessary skills can arise. The

3. The role of character in understanding the conditions for blameworthiness is discussed by Richard B. Brandt, "Blameworthiness and Obligation," in A. I. Melden, ed., *Essays in Moral Philosophy* (Seattle: University of Washington Press, 1958). See also Joel Feinberg, "Action and Responsibility," in Max Black, ed., *Philosophy in America* (Ithaca, N.Y.: Cornell University Press, 1965).

question whether or not one is to be a human being does not arise. Once it is established that something is a human excellence, the question whether it is worth having for a human being is settled.

Skills and virtues, then, share this feature: the actions that are fully characteristic of these states are always in a certain respect good actions that reflect credit upon the agent. That is, the fact that his action is fully characteristic of a skill or a virtue is sufficient grounds for praising *him*, if one is so inclined. Of course, such acts may be thoroughly deplorable in other respects. Actions that are fully characteristic of *other* action-states such as strength, sight, liking to sail, or depression may not be meritorious in any respect whatever. This, then, is what marks off excellences from other action-states.

4. *Skills and Virtues*

It was not naive of Plato and Aristotle to lump together skills and virtues and to treat them as though they are the same sort of thing. Insofar as they are excellences, they are the same sort of thing. It would be naive, however, not to see immediately that skills and virtues are in important ways different. Aristotle, of course, was aware of important differences among excellences. He divided human excellences into the "moral" and "intellectual," and this division corresponds in a way to the distinction between virtues and skills. His account of the difference between these is very brief: "Intellectual virtue in the main owes both its birth and its growth to teaching (for which reason it requires experience and time), while moral virtue comes about as a result of habit" (*NE*, II, 1, 1103a15–17).

The Aristotelian "intellectual" excellences are either skills or complexes that involve skills. A skill is a capacity to do something well in the sense of doing it *proficiently*. Proficiency involves the mastery of a technique, the mastery of something that is technically difficult. The actions that a skill is the capacity to do well are things that are difficult to do well—at the very least, difficult at first for most people. An action may be difficult to do because it is painful, tedious, tiring, embarrassing, costly, or because one is, for some other reason, disinclined to do it. Sometimes an action that takes skill is difficult in one or more of these ways. This, however, is not the sort of difficulty that is an essential feature of acts characteristic of skills. The sort of difficulty that a skill is the capacity to overcome—technical difficulty—is not some contrary inclination that opposes the action. Rather, the difficulty is inherent in the doing of the action itself. In some cases, the technical difficulty is due to the complexity of the action, as in cooking or theorizing. There is much one must know in order to do these things. In other cases, however, such as hitting a baseball or performing eye surgery, the action is hard because of the coordination required. Still other actions are hard because their performance requires a complex set of reflexes, as in riding a bicycle or typing rapidly and accurately.

What those difficulties, which skills are capacities to overcome, have in common with one another is that they can be surmounted by instruction and learning. What is learned in these cases is a technique, and instruction in a technique may take the form of verbal instructions, demonstrations, diagrams, and leading the trainee through the action. The training through which skills are inculcated consists in instruction in techniques. If sight required instruction and practice to develop properly in human beings, sight would be a skill. To the extent that a child teaches himself to walk by experimentation and practice, the ability to walk is a skill. What makes an ability to act a skill is that the actions characteristic of it are difficult in a way that can be overcome by instruction in techniques and by practice that leads to proficiency. A skill is an ability that generally is learned.

Not just any ability to act that is acquired through repetition is a skill. An aspiring Sisyphus, finding he is not strong enough to roll huge stones, might acquire the requisite strength through rolling smaller stones, working gradually up to the huge ones. Insofar as he lacks strength alone, and not boulder-rolling technique, his practice is not self-teaching, his acquisition of the ability to roll the large stones is not learning, and his ability is not a skill. It is interesting and a bit puzzling to compare this with the acquisition of the ability to type without looking at the keyboard.

Here, one does learn, and the result is a skill. Yet this sort of acquisition of an ability seems no more cerebral than the acquisition of the strength to roll a boulder. Why should one acquisition be learning and the other not? Why is only one of these abilities a skill? One answer is this: rolling a stone is not technically difficult at all—the difficulty of rolling a heavy stone is not *in the action* in the way that technical difficulty would be. One can acquire the ability to roll stones— i.e., the requisite strength, thus overcoming the difficulty, by doing things quite unrelated to the action of rolling stones. One can do isometric exercises, lift weights, wrestle, or climb mountains and thereby acquire the strength to roll large stones. It is clear that in doing these things, one is not mastering any intricacies of the action of rolling stones. One cannot in this way acquire the ability to type.

A technique, then, is a sort of action that is inherently difficult in a way peculiar to itself—technically difficult. A skill is the mastery of such a technique, and it is something that *generally* is acquired through learning—through instruction and practice. Virtues are not masteries of techniques; technique has very little to do with being brave, generous, or honest, nor do these necessarily involve being proficient at any particular thing. Some virtues involve being able to do difficult things, but the difficulties involved are due to contrary inclinations, not to technical difficulties in the actions themselves.

Gilbert Ryle contrasts knowing how to do something with what he calls "knowing the difference between right and wrong."[4] As knowing how to do something consists in possessing a certain skill, "knowing the difference between right and wrong" seems for Ryle to consist in possessing certain virtues, though he is not explicit about this. He notes that while one who knows how to do something might forget how to do it, someone who knows the difference between right and wrong cannot be said to forget the difference. People do not cease to be honest, unselfish, patient, brave or generous by forgetting how to be honest, etc. One can lose a skill in this way, but not a virtue. Ryle suggests the follow-

4. "On Forgetting the Difference between Right and Wrong," in A. I. Melden, ed., *Essays in Moral Philosophy*, pp. 147–159.

ing explanation. Honesty, for example, is a matter of taking certain things seriously—a matter of caring about certain things. To cease to be honest would be a matter of coming to care less or ceasing to care—a change of heart rather than a loss of information or the loss of a skill through forgetting how to do something.

Honesty involves taking seriously certain rights and obligations, and a kind person cares about the happiness and well-being of others, but such virtues as courage, patience, and restraint do not necessarily involve caring about any *particular* sort of thing. Still, people do not forget how to be courageous or controlled. The reason is not that there is a motivational component to these things that cannot be lost by forgetting. The reason why one cannot forget how to be brave or honest is like the reason why one cannot forget how to see or how to be strong: there is no "how to" to these things. That is, virtues—all of them—like sight, strength, and health, are not skills. They do not involve technique, and thus one cannot forget how to act in accordance with them.

An agent's skill makes his action good and it makes *him* good in a certain respect. Why is the possession of such a capacity grounds for credit and praise for the agent? Many things that people want and need can be obtained only by means that are technically difficult. Because of the importance of mastery of such difficulties and the expenditure of time and effort necessary to achieve mastery, such capacities are prized. It is also a fact that we find technically difficult things inherently interesting. It is difficult to endure pain, to fast, to resist temptation, but few people seek out such difficulties because they find it interesting and enjoyable simply to overcome the difficulties. This is exactly what we do, however, in the case of the technically difficult. Besides prizing the ability to do the technically difficult because it is useful, we prize it also for its own sake.

5. Acts Fully Characteristic of Skills

An excellence, according to Aristotle, "brings into good condition the thing of which it is the excellence and makes the work of that thing be done well." What exactly is the relationship between a good action or performance, the credit due the agent for the good action, and the excellence that is the capacity or tendency to do such good actions? In every case, whatever the excellence is, whether the agent's action reflects credit upon him can be seen as some function of the relation of his action to the excellence. For some excellences, both whether the agent's action is meritorious in the relevant aspect and whether his action reflects credit upon him depend upon whether he actually possesses the relevant excellence. This is always the case with skills.

A skill is the capacity at will to perform a certain sort of action well in the sense of performing the action proficiently. Proficiency in the action is a matter of successfully overcoming the technical difficulty inherent in the action, thereby being able with some regularity to achieve the desired result efficiently and economically. A particular action will be characteristic of a certain skill if the action satisfies the standards of proficiency for actions of that kind. The relevant standards of proficiency, of course, will vary with the kind of action. Also, there are degrees of skill, and that standard by which a particular performance properly is judged is often relative to the degree of experience of the agent. There are often different standards for a beginner and for an expert, and what is a good performance for a beginner is apt to be a poor performance for someone more advanced. For the sake of simplicity, I will ignore the complexities introduced by the amount of the agent's experience in determining the standard according to which his performances are to be judged. I will assume that when a skill is mentioned, the degree of skill is understood. When I refer to standards of proficiency by which a certain action is being judged, I will assume that these standards are appropriate both for the kind of action in question and for the experience of the agent.

Consider the example of a particular act of speaking, which is characteristic of (a certain degree of) grammatical skill. The act consists in producing at a normal conversational rate several complex sentences in accordance with the rules of grammar.

Clearly, the fact that the act is characteristic of grammatical skill in this way is not sufficient for the act to reflect credit upon the speaker as a grammatical speaker. That the speaker's sentences are well constructed does not necessarily indicate that *he* deserves any credit for speaking well. It may be that the sentences accord with the rules of grammar by chance or that the sentences were constructed for the speaker by someone else. What is needed to make an act characteristic of a skill also an act for which the agent deserves credit is that the agent have the requisite skill and that his act satisfy the criteria of a good performance of that kind, not by chance or because of another's skill, but *because of* the agent's skill. For a speech to be *fully* characteristic of skill at speaking grammatically, the fact that the sentences uttered conform to the rules of grammar must be directly attributable to the agent's skill. One might also want to cite the agent's effort or particularly favorable circumstances in explaining why the act is up to a certain standard. To reflect credit upon the agent as a grammatical speaker, however, his speaking grammatically must be explained, at least in part, by the fact that he possesses the requisite skill. In this case, his excellence *makes* his speaking grammatically good and it makes him a good grammatical speaker. If an action is characteristic of a skill, but the action's satisfying the criteria of proficiency is not due to the agent's possessing the requisite skill, then the "skillfulness" of the act does not reflect credit upon the agent, and the act is not fully characteristic of the skill. Skill at speaking grammatically is not the capacity to utter grammatical sentences that have been constructed by others. Rather, it is the capacity to construct and utter such sentences oneself.

In summary: assume that an action performed by a certain agent meets standards of proficiency, P. The skill, S, is a capacity at will to perform actions that meet P. This action is characteristic of skill S (by hypothesis). The action will be fully characteristic of skill S just in case the action meets standard P *because* the agent possesses skill S. The circumstances that would make it *inappropriate* to credit the agent for his action's meeting P would be any circumstances that indicate that the agent's possession of the requisite skill was not among the conditions that explain why the action meets standards *P*.

More complicated is the question of what is required to fault an agent for a performance that is not up to standards of proficiency. By *faulting* an agent for something he has done, I mean the opposite counterpart of crediting him for an action. In this sense, to fault an agent for doing something is to judge that his action in some way reflects discredit upon him, that it reflects poorly upon him. So, for example, if someone speaks ungrammatically, and I judge that this poor performance reflects adversely upon him as a grammatical speaker, I have faulted him as a grammatical speaker for his poor performance. What I seek here is an account of the conditions that make such a judgment true.

I will argue subsequently that for some kinds of acting badly, faulting the agent for the bad action comes to the same thing as judging that his action is fully characteristic of some vice—some bad character trait. Not all excellences have opposite action-states that are bad, however, and this is true of skills. Skills are simply capacities to do things that are technically difficult, and the "opposite" of a skill is only its absence. When a performance is poor because it falls short of the appropriate standard of proficiency, then the question whether the agent is to be faulted for the poor performance often becomes the question whether there is an explanation of the action's not being up to standards, which explanation is consistent with the agent's having the skill to meet the standards. Roughly, the agent's having the requisite skill to speak grammatically consists in the fact that in normal circumstances, he can at will speak in accordance with the rules of grammar at a normal conversational rate. If a certain speech is ungrammatical, this performance will not necessarily reflect adversely upon the speaker if, for example, it is established that he was not trying to speak grammatically—perhaps he was speaking ungrammatically on purpose. Or perhaps he was drugged or very tired. It is presupposed in these cases that there is some evidence

that the agent has the requisite skill. When there is no reason to
suppose that someone has any skill at golfing, the fact that he
makes a very poor score on a particular afternoon is perfectly
consistent with what one would expect, and it is not apt to be
attributed to his not trying or his being tired. On the other hand,
if Arnold Palmer fails to break 100, if Bobby Fischer loses to a
beginner in twelve moves, or if W. V. Quine commits five
elementary mistakes in reasoning in a single lecture, there is an
enormous presumption that some special explanation makes it
inappropriate to fault the agent on the basis of his ability. Such
explanations are *excuses* for a poor performance. This is not to say
that the poor performance is not the agent's fault. If a skilled
dancer performs poorly because he is not trying, one cannot fault
him as a *skilled dancer*. That he did not try is an excuse that
makes *this* faulting judgment inappropriate. If he should have
tried, however—if, for instance, he had contracted to dance
skillfully—then he is not keeping his agreement, and he might be
faulted for this. Another circumstance, such as a severe muscular
cramp during the performance, might serve to block *both* faulting
judgments and preserve unblemished his technical reputation
and his character.

Suppose, then, that an action performed by an agent is judged
by standards of proficiency P and fails to meet those standards.
Again, the skill, S, is the capacity at will to perform actions that
meet P. In this case the action is not characteristic of S. It will be
correct to fault the agent for his action's failing to meet P just in
case the action falls short of P because the agent does not possess
the requisite skill, S.

The circumstances that would make it inappropriate to fault
the agent with respect to his skill for a poor technical performance
would be any circumstances indicating that his action's not being
up to standards is due to something other than his not possessing
the requisite skill. Excuses here are *other* explanations of the
failure.

Doing well, then, in the sense of doing proficiently, reflects
credit upon the agent only if the agent does well because he

possesses the requisite skill. One consequence of this point is that one cannot gradually acquire a certain level of skill by performing a number of acts *fully* characteristic of that level of skill. This is not to say that it is impossible to learn—to acquire the skill—by doing. It does imply, however, that it is impossible gradually to acquire a certain level of skill by repeatedly doing well at that level. This point needs to be kept in mind in considering how skills and virtues are acquired.

6. *The Acquisition of Excellences*

Acquiring an excellence, be it a skill or a virtue, is not only acquiring a capacity or tendency to act in a certain way; it is also a matter of acquiring merit. It would seem that merit accrues to an agent as the result of his doing well. If, however, one thinks of an excellence as what *makes* both an agent and his action good, then a problem arises about how an agent accumulates merit in the first place—how he acquires the excellence. Aristotle addressed himself to some such problem as this, but it is not clear what his solution was. The matter is complicated by the fact that actions fully characteristic of skills are related to skills differently from the relation of actions fully characteristic of virtues to virtues. Indeed, the virtues exhibit considerable diversity from one another in this respect.

Aristotle formulated the problem in this way. "The question might be asked, what we mean by saying that we must become just by doing just acts... ; for if men do just... acts, they are already just..., exactly as, if they do what is in accordance with the laws of grammar..., they are grammarians" (1105a17–21).

In response to this question, Aristotle makes the following points.

(a) It is possible for someone who has no grammatical skill "to do something in accordance with the laws of grammar, either by chance or at the suggestion of another" (1105a22–23).

(b) Skills and virtues differ in that with a skill all that matters is that the product "have a certain character." The skill is the capacity to produce a product "having a certain character"

(1105a27–28).[5] A virtue, however, is not just the capacity to do acts having a certain character. It does not follow from the fact that the acts have a certain character that they are "done justly or temperately" (1105a29–30).

(c) "The agent also must be in a certain condition when he does them [acts done temperately or justly]; in the first place he must have knowledge, secondly he must choose the acts, and choose them for their own sakes, and thirdly his action must proceed from a firm and unchangeable character" (1105a31–35).

Aristotle obviously does not mean that a "just act" *must* proceed from the firm and unchangeable character of *being a just person*. This interpretation would directly contradict his claim that we become just by doing just acts. The three conditions in the passage cited in (c) above must be understood as conditions for a *just man's acting justly*. That is, they are conditions for an action's exhibiting the agent's justice. Aristotle's point can be put in this way: a skill is simply the capacity to produce acts of a certain character (i.e., conforming to a certain standard of proficiency). A virtue is a capacity and tendency to act in ways that meet the three conditions of knowledge, motive, and proceeding from fixed character. This interpretation is borne out by the very next sentence after the statement of the three conditions. "These are not reckoned in as conditions of the possession of the arts, except the bare knowledge; but *as a condition of the possession of the virtues* knowledge has little or no weight, while the other conditions count not for a little but for everything, i.e., the very conditions which result from often doing just and temperate acts" (1105a35–b5, my emphasis).

A distinction is made between a "just act" and an "act done justly." An act done justly must satisfy the three conditions in (c) above; it must be an act that exhibits the agent's justice—it must

5. Aristotle is thinking here of an "art"—a skill of *making something*, where the final product is an artifact. His point, however, is easily adapted to skills the exercise of which does not produce an artifact—skill at dancing or acrobatics, for example. Here, Aristotle might say that all that matters is that the *action* have a certain character.

be done by a just person acting justly. This is comparable to an act *done skillfully*. Such an act can be done only by someone who possesses the requisite skill, and, therefore, every skillful act also exhibits the agent's skill. A *just act* (as distinguished from an act done justly) need not fulfill the third condition in (c). There is, then, no inconsistency in holding that someone who is not a just person might gradually become a just person by doing just acts. It is not clear, however, what a just act is. Must it fulfill the *motive* condition in (c)? Or is it enough that the action be of a certain character—that it be what a just person acting justly would do? The answer to this question is crucial for understanding Aristotle's account of how the *aretai ēthikai* are acquired.

Perhaps this is the account Aristotle would give of how a virtue is acquired: children are offered inducements in the form of rewards and punishments to act justly. Eventually, if all goes well, they acquire the requisite knowledge, motivation, and permanent dispostion that make them just people.[6]

Aristotle might have meant, however, that it is by performing meritorious just actions—acts fully characteristic of the virtue, justice—that one acquires the virtue. Although it is not possible to perform an act fully characteristic of a skill without actually possessing the skill, it is not clear that this is the case with virtues. In those cases in which a certain virtue is a *tendency* to act in a certain way, there is no reason why someone who lacks the virtue cannot act in a way *fully characteristic* of that virtue. If this is so, then we might entertain the hypothesis that at least some virtues are acquired by performing actions fully characteristic of them. It is by no means clear that this is what Aristotle meant. It might not have occurred to him that virtues differ from skills

6. In *Aristotle's Ethical Theory*, pp. 104–107, W. F. R. Hardie defends this both as an interpretation of Aristotle and as a hypothesis about the acquisition of virtues. There is some reason to doubt that this hypothesis is true. See Lawrence Kohlberg, "Development of Moral Character and Moral Ideology," in M. L. Hoffman and L. W. Hoffman, eds., *Review of Child Development Research*, I (New York: Russell Sage Foundation, 1964), 388–389.

in that it is possible for someone who does not possess a virtue to act in a way fully characteristic of the virtue.

7. *Acts Fully Characteristic of Virtues and Vices*

The relation of a character trait to the acts fully characteristic of it is apt to be different from the relation of a skill to the acts that exhibit it. Also, there are considerable differences among the virtues themselves. For purposes of illustration, I will discuss some aspects of the relation of the virtue truthfulness to the actions fully characteristic of it. For several reasons, truthfulness is more manageable than certain other character traits. Truthfulness is a species of conscientiousness; it belongs to the same family as honesty, fairness, and being a person of one's word. Truthfulness is less like such virtues as courage, kindness, and generosity. Caution is in order, therefore, in treating truthfulness as a "typical" virtue. Also, fundamental disagreements about ethics may lead to differing conceptions of truthfulness. The following account sketches what I take to be a very common conception of truthfulness. The trait described really is a virtue, I believe, but the justification of this view belongs in the discussion of conscientiousness in a subsequent chapter.

In the case of skills, an act characteristic of a skill can be defined as an act that meets certain standards of proficiency, and this act can be contrasted with an act *fully* characteristic of the skill, which not only meets these standards but is also such that it reflects credit upon the agent. In the difference between an act *fully* characteristic of a skill and an act that is merely characteristic of the skill lie the conditions for personal merit, the conditions for crediting the agent for the proficiency of his action. It is useful to make a similar contrast between an act merely characteristic of a virtue (or vice) and an act *fully* characteristic of the trait. Truthfulness, however, is not a matter of meeting any standards of proficiency. It is possible to stipulate at the outset the features that an action must have in order to be an action characteristic of truthfulness. It seems more straightforward, however, to adopt a different strategy and to begin instead with an account of an action *fully* characteristic of truthfulness.

A truthful person, of course, is one noted for telling the truth. It is obviously not necessary for being a truthful person that one always tell the truth as one sees it. There are times when one should not tell the truth, and it would not necessarily count against one's being a truthful person if one remained silent or prevaricated on such occasions. It is obvious too that not every act of intentional truth-telling exhibits truthfulness. The telling of true anecdotes and the passing on of true information in conversation, in circumstances in which there is no reason to suppress the truth, do not exhibit truthfulness. To begin with, then, we can expect that a truthful person is one who tells the truth when he should even though he has some reason not to.

It is important to us that we be able to count upon one another to tell the truth in certain situations and not knowingly to mislead. We seek to inculcate and to reinforce the attitude that refraining from withholding the truth or from lying in such circumstances is important for its own sake. We hold that it is wrong to lie in such circumstances without some special justification. Sometimes it is contrary to a person's inclinations or immediate interests to tell the truth, and it is to his liking or his advantage to mislead others. When an individual is so disinclined, it is often difficult for him to tell the truth. The stronger his disinclination to tell the truth, the more difficult this may be for him.

Truthfulness, then, is the firm disposition to tell the truth when one should. This firm disposition is exhibited when a person, having reason not to tell the truth because it would advance his own interests or suit his own inclinations not to do so, instead tells the truth because he thinks he should. Actions that exhibit this trait, then, will have the following characteristics.

(1) The agent communicates something he believes to be true.

(2) The agent believes that it is somehow contrary to his own interests or inclinations to tell what he tells.

(3) The agent communicates what he takes to be the truth

56

because he believes that in such circumstances it is wrong to mislead others, and he wants to avoid doing such a wrong.

It may also be necessary for such an act that some or all of the beliefs of the agent mentioned in these three conditions be true or, at least, in some sense, reasonable. These conditions, however, are the most salient and important ones for present purposes. It is apparent, I think, that an act fully characteristic of truthfulness might be performed by someone who is not a truthful person. Someone who genuinely believes that it is generally wrong to mislead others to suit one's inclinations or to promote one's own advantage might, at the same time, be greedy and weak. He might, then, with some regularity lie to others and subsequently feel guilty about so doing. Such a person does not have a firm (enough) disposition to tell the truth when he should. Still, he might on some occasion resolve to speak truthfully and then win the struggle with himself. His act would satisfy the conditions for an act fully characteristic of truthfulness as set out above, and this seems right, since such an action would reflect credit upon the agent. That is, his speaking truthfully is commendable, and he deserves some degree of praise for so doing.

Someone can perform an act fully characteristic of truthfulness, then, without possessing the excellence, truthfulness. For an act to *exhibit* the excellence, truthfulness, however, not only must the action fulfill the three conditions above, but, to use Aristotle's phrase, "his action must proceed from a firm and unchangeable character" (1105a34–35)—that is, the agent must have a pretty firm resolve to tell the truth when he should, and he must have the strength of will to hold to his resolve even when his own interests or inclinations bid him to lie or to suppress the truth. We might distinguish two sorts of liars. One would simply lack any commitment to telling the truth for its own sake and therefore see no reason why in general he should tell the truth when this runs counter to his interests or inclinations. The other sort might have such a commitment, but be sufficiently greedy, self-serving, or self-indulgent that the latter desires predominate.

Perhaps much lying results from both an insufficiently strong desire to tell the truth and excessively strong contrary desires and inclinations.

Whenever someone tells the truth or what he takes to be the truth in circumstances in which there exists some reason for him to lie or where he believes that there is such a reason, his action will be characteristic of truthfulness. His action will be *fully* characteristic of this virtue provided that it also satisfies the motive and "knowledge" conditions set out in conditions (1)–(3) above. Finally, the action will *exhibit* the virtue truthfulness only if the agent has the proper sort of resolve generally to tell the truth when he should and the strength of will to act on the resolve. Only in the last case must the agent actually have the virtue. In the case of truthfulness, then, the agent need not be a truthful person in order to speak truthfully in a way that reflects credit upon him. In order for the act to reflect credit upon him, however, the act must be of the sort that the virtue truthfulness is the tendency to perform. The excellence, then, is still central to the account of the relation between action and personal merit, though the relation is different from that which holds with skills and the actions fully characteristic of them.

Most virtues have at least one opposite vice, in contrast to skills, which have no such opposite states. Faulting an agent for an action that falls short of a standard of proficiency is a matter of ruling out any explanation of the failure other than *the lack* of the requisite skill. One way of faulting an agent for an action, however, is to establish that the action is fully characteristic of some vice. For instance, to fault someone for failing to tell the truth when he should, it is sufficient to show that his failure is fully characteristic of mendacity.

In its psychological structure, mendacity is the mirror image of truthfulness, being a deficiency in commitment to telling the truth or the inability to subordinate other desires to the desire to be truthful. Mendacity will manifest itself as the tendency to lie when it appears to be a means of satisfying one's own inclinations or interests. The actions fully characteristic of this vice, then, will be done with the intent of misleading people. As with truthfulness, one need not be a mendacious person to act in a way fully characteristic of mendacity. On the other hand, not every action that involves a failure to tell the truth when the agent should will be fully characteristic of mendacity. The agent may be mistaken about what the truth is, or he may be ignorant of certain particulars that make it wrong for him not to tell the truth.

It is a plausible thesis generally that the faulty actions philosophers lump under the heading of "morally wrong" are actions fully characteristic of some vice, and that excuses which mitigate or remove fault are factors which show that the action does not satisfy some condition for actions fully characteristic of some vice. A corollary may be that there exist some vices for which we have no names. This is not to say that every action fully characteristic of some vice is "morally wrong." There is a disagreement about the extension of the term 'moral,' and several issues of substance are involved in these differences.

Treating virtues as species of the genus excellences emphasizes the crucial relation of such states to the merit of both actions and agents. When we consider in any detail, however, what some of these states are and why they are prized, it is apparent that there is considerable diversity among these states. It is not surprising that we should prize a variety of states of people. One result of considering excellences in general, however, is this: If we seek an explanation of why certain features of a particular action are relevant to its being a good (or bad) action, its reflecting credit (or discredit) upon the agent, we would do well to consider the hypothesis that those features are connected with the action's being fully characteristic of some excellence (or vice), which we prize (or despise). The explanation of why the feature is relevant to the evaluation of the action may be found in the account of the nature and value of the particular virtue or vice involved. The latter, in turn, may be understood in terms of the role or roles that the trait plays in human life generally. Things may become visible from this perspective that are not readily apparent from other perspectives.

III

Courage, Cowardice, and Self-Indulgence

Desires and aversions of various kinds can disrupt an individual's practical reasoning or prevent it from issuing in action. There are certain virtues whose function is to forestall such disruptions and interferences. Among these virtues are courage, even-temperedness, patience, and a virtue that is the opposite of self-indulgence. The Greeks called this last virtue *sōphrosunē*, but there seems to be no single word in English for the opposite of self-indulgence, and thus no single word which adequately translates the Greek word. The best we seem able to do is "temperance," which is archaic, or such terms as "self-control" or "restraint" which are less specific than "*sōphrosunē*."

R. B. Brandt has defended what he calls the "motivational theory" of character traits, the view that "traits [of character] are dispositions of the want/aversion kind." Anticipating the objection that such traits as courage do not involve any particular characteristic wants or aversions, Brandt points out that some traits can be viewed as the absence of an opposite trait that is itself a dispostion of the want/aversion variety. Fear, for example, is an aversion, and a coward is someone who is disposed to act in certain situations from the motive fear. Courage, the polar opposite of cowardice, is not a disposition to act from a particular type of motive. Rather, it is the absence of the coward's disposition to act from fear.[1]

From the perspective of a motivational theory of character traits, courage and such other virtues as even-temperedness, patience, and *sōphrosunē* are privative states. Their polar opposite vices are tendencies to act in certain situations from certain types of motives, while these virtues are the absence of such tendencies.

This account conforms to certain facts, but it is incomplete. More can be said about these virtues; they have a positive aspect. Courage and restraint are found in people who do have fears and desires and who do from time to time act at the promptings of these. The opposite vices—cowardice and self-indulgence—are dispositions to act from such motives *in certain situations*. The situations in question are, roughly, those in which the agent *should not* act as these motives lead him to act. Thus, although these virtues can be regarded as privative states from the standpoint of motivational theory, they reveal a positive aspect when one considers their relation to practical reason. One might say, then, that these virtues are the positive capacity for acting rationally when certain motives are apt to incline us to do otherwise. An account of those traits must attend both to the motives that are essential constituents of the vices and to the relationship of these motives to practical reason.

Such considerations lead to the view that these virtues and vices concern the conflict of reason and desire, where "desire" is to be understood in a very broad sense that comprises wants, aversions, inclinations, cravings, appetites, and emotions. This conflict, of course, is the basis for the ancient and compelling view that each person has a rational element or part and a distinct desiring part (or parts). There are a variety of accounts of the sense in which these are elements or parts. With this model in

1. "Traits of Character: A Conceptual Analysis," *American Philosophical Quarterly*, 7 (1970), 23–37.

the background, it is very natural to conceive certain virtues as the ability of the rational part to control the desiring part(s). We thus become concerned with the authoritativeness of the rational element and the tractability of the desires. It is against the background of such metaphors that we understand the thesis that the function of courage, *sōphrosunē*, etc., is the preservation of practical reason when it conflicts with certain desires. Consider, for example, Thomas Aquinas's view of "fortitude." "The passions withdraw us from following the dictate of reason, e.g., through fear of danger or toil, and then man needs to be strengthened for that which reason dictates, lest he turn back, and to this end there is fortitude" (*Summa Theologiae* I–II, Q. 61, Art. 2).

The view that these virtues determine the outcome between two struggling elements has its element of truth and its point. If it is taken to suffice as a philosophical account, however, it is an unsatisfactory one. To begin with, it will not account for all manifestations of these virtues and vices, because sometimes there is no struggle. Moreover, the separation and compartmentalization of the reasoning part and the desiring part, if taken literally, makes it impossible to understand either. How can pure intellect speak to mindless craving? This problem is avoided by anthropomorphizing these parts or elements—a person is regarded as a committee of individuals, one member taking the part of reason and another the part of desire. This once again is metaphor. Moreover, when we are trying to understand how an individual's desires and reasoning interact in order to explain the nature and merit or demerit of certain traits, it is not illuminating to be told that it is as if each person were several people who reason and desire and struggle with one another. This is the very sort of thing we seek to understand. There is the further danger that we will also attribute to these metaphorical individuals the very virtues and vices we are trying to explain.

Some remarks of John Dewey suggest another way of conceiving the relation between reason and desire.

It is notorious that some moralists have deplored the influence of desire; they have found the heart of strife between good and evil in the conflict of desire with reason, in which the former has force on its side and the latter authority. But reasonableness is in fact a quality of an effective relationship among desires rather than a thing opposed to desire. It signifies the order, perspective, proportion which is achieved, during deliberation, out of a diversity of earlier incompatible preferences. Choice is reasonable when it induces us to act reasonably; that is, with regard to the claims of each of the competing habits and impulses.[2]

Still, courage, self-control, restraint, etc., have to do in some way with the preservation of practical reason when it is in opposition to certain emotions and desires. Dewey's view is a useful reminder that reason and desire cannot be understood independently of one another. It helps us to be wary of certain inadequate conceptions of them to which we are particularly susceptible, conceptions that prevent us from seeing how they interact. A study of these virtues and vices should provide some positive account of how they do interact.

1. Two Views of Cowardice and Courage

It is generally difficult to do things one believes to be dangerous, more difficult for some than others. Of course, it is fear that makes this difficult. It sometimes happens, however, that the considerations in favor of a dangerous course of action make it seem worth the risks. People are sometimes able to act in the face of such dangers, but sometimes they are deterred. It might be that as the moment to act approaches, one's fear grows, and one becomes irresolute. Joseph Conrad, in Chapter 1 of *Lord Jim*, describes such a moment for a young man who dreamed of acts of unflinching heroism. Jim is a student on a training-ship anchored in a harbor.

He was jostled. "Man the cutter!" Boys rushed past him. A coaster running in for shelter had crashed through a schooner at anchor, and one of the ship's instructors had seen the accident. A mob of boys clambered on the rails, clustered round the davits. "Collision. Just ahead of us. Mr. Symons saw it." A push made him stagger against the

2. John Dewey, *Human Nature and Conduct* (New York: Holt, 1922), pp. 194–195.

mizzen-mast, and he caught hold of a rope. The old training-ship chained to her moorings quivered all over, bowing gently head to wind, and with her scanty rigging humming in a deep bass the breathless song of her youth at sea. "Lower away!" He saw the boat, manned, drop swiftly below the rail, and he rushed after her. He heard a splash, "Let go; clear the falls!" He leaned over. The river alongside seethed in frothy streaks.... Jim felt his shoulder gripped firmly. "Too late, youngster."

With cases of this sort in mind, we might take courage to be the ability to act upon one's beliefs about what it is best to do when fear inclines one not to act so. On this view, courage and cowardice have to do with the *conflict* of reason with the passion, fear. The conflict is envisaged as taking place within the breast of the agent.

Consider, however, these lines by the Ionian poet, Archilochus.

Some lucky Thracian has my noble shield:
I had to run; I dropped it in a wood.
But I got clear away, thank God! So hang
The shield! I'll get another, just as good.[3]

If we assume that Archilochus's soldier is perfectly candid in what he says, then there is no conflict between what the soldier thought he should do and what fear inclined him to do. Yet one wonders whether his flight was cowardly. We need to know more about the circumstances to decide this. The lack of conflict between reason and fear in the soldier, however, does not seem to rule out the possibility that his act was cowardly.

On another view, a view allowing the possibility that Archilochus's soldier is a coward, courage is necessary in dangerous situations for proper practical reasoning. That is, where danger is involved, for properly grounded belief about what course of action is best, one needs courage. A coward, on the other hand, is someone whose practical reasoning is defective in a certain way. In his deliberations, he gives too much weight to dangers to himself and as a result makes wrong decisions. One might say

3. The lines are quoted by H. D. F. Kitto in *The Greeks* (Baltimore: Penguin Books, 1951), p. 88.

with Plato that a coward is ignorant of what is and what is not truly dangerous, and consequently he makes errors in weighing and measuring goods and evils in deliberating (*Protagoras*, 360 B–D).

On the first view of courage and cowardice, which I shall call the "Kantian" view (with apologies to Kant), a coward is prevented by fear from doing what he thinks best. Courage is the ability to do what one's reason dictates in the face of fear. According to the Platonic view of courage and cowardice, however, the coward gives too much weight to dangers in his calculations, and therefore he is deterred from a dangerous course of action when he should not be. On this view, therefore, there is no opposition between what fear inclines him to do and the dictate of his reason. An adequate account of courage and cowardice must somehow combine elements of both of these views.

2. Cowardly Acts

The relations between practical reason and fear are most easily seen in cowardly acts. It is instructive to take an ordinary uncomplicated act and consider what would have to be the case in order for the act to be fully characteristic of the vice cowardice. Suppose that a man named Smith stayed home today and his staying home was cowardly. It would have to be that his staying home today is incompatible with his doing something else that he has some reason to do. It would also have to be that he knows or imagines that there is danger involved in doing this other thing or at least that he is afraid to do it.

These two conditions are clearly not sufficient for the man's staying at home to be cowardly. Suppose he is a steeplejack staying home from work. Here, his staying home is incompatible with his going to work, and he has some interest in going to work. His work is dangerous. Still, he might be staying home because he is sick or because he is lazy, and in such a case his staying home would not be cowardly. It would seem necessary to add that he is staying home rather than going to work because he is afraid to go to work.

Still, however, the description that has been given of Smith's staying home does not necessarily indicate that his staying at home is cowardly. Suppose that his employer has altered working conditions so that Smith's work now involves a great deal of danger, and he is now staying at home because he is afraid to work under such conditions. Suppose that he is now expected to climb towers that are in danger of collapsing. It might be that he believes that working under such conditions is simply not worth the risk involved. Perhaps he does not need his present job enough to warrant taking such risks. If so, his staying home rather than going to work would not necessarily be cowardly.

From the foregoing, we might extract the following tentative list of necessary conditions for A's doing X to be cowardly:

There must be some action Y such that

(1) A is doing X rather than Y.

(2) A believes that he has some reason to do Y.

(3) A is doing X rather than Y because he is afraid to do Y.

(4) A does not believe that his doing Y is not worth the risk it involves.

That these four conditions are necessary conditions for a cowardly act is supported by the fact that if A does X rather than Y, and is accused of cowardice for this, A generally can turn aside the charge of cowardice if he can establish any one of the following.

(a) A saw no reason whatever to do Y.

(b) A's reason for doing X rather than Y was not that he was afraid to do Y; rather it was something else.

(c) A did X rather than Y because he was afraid to do Y, but A believed that the risks involved in doing Y were not worth whatever good would be accomplished by doing Y.

Defense (a) entails the absence of necessary condition (2). Defense (b) entails the absence of (3). The latter is the sort of defense that a conscientious objector would be entitled to offer against the charge of cowardice. He might admit that he finds frightening the prospect of fighting, but that it is because of moral scruples about hurting people rather than fear of being hurt himself that he refused to fight. There are often difficulties in actual cases in establishing that the facts that correspond to (a) and (b) actually obtain. Once established, however, those defenses effectively defeat the charge of cowardice.

Condition (4) and defense (c), which entails the falsity of (4), concern the relation of practical reasoning and fear. If one takes the "Kantian" view that cowardice is a matter of fear overcoming an agent's practical reason, then one will expect that something like (4) is a necessary condition for a cowardly act. If from the start, both the agent's fear and his practical reasoning incline him in the same direction, there is no question of one overcoming the other. On the other hand, one might want to allow for the possibility that at least some cowardly acts result from an agent's giving danger to himself too much weight in his practical reasoning. If this is so, then (4) is not a necessary condition for a cowardly act, and there is at least some truth in the Platonic view.

Clearly *some* cowardly acts are cases of fear leading someone to act contrary to what he thinks he should do, and in these cases condition (4) is satisfied. In Conrad's *Lord Jim*, Jim's desertion from the *Patna*, a ship full of Moslem pilgrims for whose safety he was responsible, is one such case. The intensity of Jim's shame and remorse for his desertion shows that he believed that he should have stayed with the ship, yet he left because he was afraid for his life. This is one such case. Are there no cowardly acts where, although conditions (1)–(3) are fulfilled, the agent believes that doing Y is *not* worth the risk it involves? Jim was not the only officer of the *Patna* to desert the damaged ship and its passengers. The captain of the ship and some other members of the crew, whose duty lay with the ship as much as did Jim's, deserted also. Their crime, however, seems to have been something other than cowardice. In Chapter II, Conrad describes the passengers as they board the *Patna* at the start of the voyage.

They came covered with dust, with sweat, with grime, with rags—the strong men at the head of family parties, the lean old men pressing forward without hope of return; young boys with fearless eyes glancing curiously, shy little girls with tumbled long hair; the timid women muffled up and clasping to their breasts, wrapped in loose ends of soiled headcloths, their sleeping babies, the unconscious pilgrims of an exacting belief.

The reaction of the captain of the *Patna* to this scene is "Look at dese cattle." From this and other comments, it is clear that there is no doubt in the captain's mind that his passengers are not worth the risk of his own life. When he deserted the damaged ship in the face of a storm, he left because he feared for his life, but his desertion is due not to cowardice but to his callous indifference to his passengers and his indifference to the responsibilities of his position.

The case of the *Patna*'s captain appears to support the view that (c) is a defense against cowardice and therefore the view that (4) is a necessary condition for a cowardly act. There are, however, two crucially different types of cases that fail to satisfy condition (4). One type of case, exemplified by the case of the *Patna*'s captain, is not cowardly action. Another type, however, may be cowardly. Consider the case of Smythe who is terribly afraid of being hurt. She is convinced that it is worth suffering any frustration and humiliation in order to avoid the danger of pain and injury. She sometimes neglects her affairs, family, and friends, not because she is indifferent, but because she is so afraid of being injured, that all other considerations pale beside the urgency of avoiding this sort of danger. Smythe's neglect of her affairs, etc., due to fear of injury might be cowardly, even though Smythe really believes that her affairs are not worth the risk of injury.[4]

In the terms of condition (4), both the captain and Smythe have weighed the relative merits of doing Y against the risks. Both have decided that doing Y is not worth the risks. The difference between the two cases lies in the agents' attitudes towards the risks involved. The captain of the *Patna* has the usual fear of injury and death, but is relatively indifferent to the considerations that indicate his remaining with his ship. Smythe, on the other hand, has the usual concern for her obligations, commitments, and

4. I am grateful to John Cooper, who persuaded me to take this sort of case seriously.

affairs but seems *excessively* concerned about the possibility of being injured. She is excessively concerned because she is excessively afraid of being injured. It is because her weighing of the merits and risks is decisively influenced by her excessive fear that Smythe's behavior is cowardly.

This example raises the problem of explaining what it is to be *excessively* afraid. Following Aristotle, we might take as the norm the individual who is good at deciding what to do—the person who is able consistently to make the right decision. *Excessive* fear would be fear that led a person to give too much weight to danger in deciding what to do—more weight than a *phronimos* (practically wise man) would give it. In the absence of an account of *phronēsis*, however, this explanation is not very satisfying.

The norm relative to which excessive fears are excessive can be explicated in terms of our conception of normal human activity. Just as being injured and being ill are essentially certain sorts of incapacities for normal activity, so too is proneness to excessive fear. The capacities involved in being healthy (that is, being neither injured nor ill) are certain sorts of capacities for engaging in activities. These capacities involve having a body that will move in certain ways, a certain degree of strength and endurance, and the absence of pain that hampers activity. Among the states of the human body that appreciably diminish these capacities are illnesses and injuries. Being prone to excessive fear is like being ill or injured in that it incapacitates one, although the nature of the incapacity is different. For one thing, the incapacity due to excessive fear may be the result of one's giving too much weight to dangers in one's practical reasoning, whereas injuries and illnesses are not incapacitating because they distort one's judgment. The cause of the former incapacity is mental, whereas the cause of the latter is physical. Being prone to excessive fear, however, is not necessarily a form of mental illness, although it may be if it becomes incapacitating enough. Just as too little strength and endurance may constitute a defect without being pronounced enough to constitute ill health, so proneness to excessive fears may fall short of being illness.

Our notion of normal human activity is extremely complex. It must be understood in terms of a way of life. More stamina and endurance are required to live as the Australian aborigines once lived than are required of the present inhabitants of Sidney or Melbourne. One would expect that certain standards for health among the aborigines would be higher than they are for us. What one should be able to do normally, however, is a familiar conception; it is bound up in our understanding of health, illness, and injury, and, I am suggesting, our understanding of cowardice and courage.

The list of necessary conditions for A's doing X being cowardly, then, must be amended to allow for cowardly acts that do not spring from an opposition between an agent's reason and his fear. The first three conditions remain as before. That is:

(i) A is doing X rather than Y.

(ii) A knows or believes that he has some reason to do Y.

(iii) A is doing X rather than Y because he is afraid to do Y.

The fourth condition, however, must allow for two different possible relations of A's fear and his practical reasoning. There are the cowardly acts in which the agent's fear opposes and leads him to act contrary to his practical reasoning. Such cases, exemplified by Conrad's Jim, support what I have called the "Kantian" account of cowardice. There appear to be cases, however, that do not fit this account, cases that seem to support the Platonic account. In these cases, the cowardly action issues from defective practical reasoning, the defect being due to excessive fear. Condition (4) for A's doing X being cowardly, then, might be reformulated as a disjunction

(iv) *Either*

A does not believe that his doing Y is not worth the risks it involves,

Or

If A does believe that his doing Y is not worth the risks involved, he believes this because he is *excessively afraid* of the risks he sees in doing Y.

According to Plato's account in the *Protagoras*, it is *ignorance* that leads a coward in his practical reasoning to give more weight than he should to certain dangers. The second disjunct of (iv)

appears to locate the difficulty in excessive fear rather than ignorance, and this may seem different from what Plato intended. If
A's doing X is cowardly, and A really believes that his doing Y is
not worth the risks it involves, then is it necessary that this belief
be due to fear? Is it really necessary for a cowardly act that the
agent's giving too much weight to dangers to himself is due to
fear? Do we not often encounter people who are cautious to the
point of cowardice from intellectual rather than emotional
causes? Suppose our Smythe had been taught as a child that
nothing is worth the risk of pain and injury to herself and that she
learned this 'prudential' precept just as she learned that one
should not harm others unnecessarily, that one should keep one's
word, etc. If this were the case, then she holds this view about
risks to herself because of teaching and training, and not because
of any feeling she has. Yet this precept leads her to act in ways
that are clearly cowardly. In this case, then, it is not fear that
distorts her practical reasoning. Rather, it is a mistaken premise.
She is, as Plato might have said, ignorant about what is most
worth while. Such cases of cowardly action seem to satisfy neither
disjunct of condition (iv), and thus (iv) is not a necessary condition for A's doing X to be cowardly.[5]

I want to say in response, however, that someone who is taught
in this way as a precept that nothing is worth pain and injury to
himself is taught thereby to be excessively afraid of pain and
injury. That the pupil never *feels* any fear during the learning
process or afterwards would be surprising, but it does not affect
the fact that he learns to be excessively afraid of pain and injury.

In thinking of fear, there is a tendency to think exclusively of
the set of physiological occurrences and feelings that accompany
panic and terror. In discussing fear, William James quoted
Charles Darwin:

The frightened man at first stands like a statue, motionless and breathless, or crouches down as if instinctively to escape observation. The
heart beats quickly and violently, so that it palpitates or knocks against
the ribs; ... the skin instantly becomes pale as during incipient faintness.... That the skin is much affected under the sense of great fear, we

5. I am indebted to Lester Hunt for this objection.

see in the marvelous manner in which perspiration immediately exudes from it.... The hairs also on the skin stand erect, and the superficial muscles shiver.... The salivary glands act imperfectly; the mouth becomes dry.... One of the best marked symptoms is the trembling of all the muscles of the body.... As fear increases into an agony of terror... the heart beats wildly or must fail to act and faintness ensue; there is a death-like pallor; the breathing is labored.... All the muscles of the body may become rigid or may be thrown into convulsive movements.[6]

James's view was that fear consists in one's feeling such physical responses as Darwin described. He came to this view because he assumed that fear is to be discovered by introspection, and these feelings were all that he could find by this means. *"If we fancy some strong emotion, and then try to abstract from our consciousness of it all the feelings of its bodily symptoms, we find we have nothing left behind,* no 'mind-stuff' out of which the emotion can be constituted."[7]

Such physical changes and the feelings that accompany them, however, are but one aspect or facet of fear, which is a far more complex and complicated phenomenon than James realized. In *Philosophical Investigations,* Wittgenstein shows that a wide variety of psychological phenomena—understanding, meaning, intending, etc.—must be understood as features of forms of life that are fundamentally social and public. The view that these things consist exclusively of "introspectibilia" necessarily leads to unsatisfactory conceptions. Fear of bears characteristically involves, in addition to a tendency to tremble and perspire when confronted by a bear, the belief that bears are dangerous, and the inclination to avoid confrontations with bears. Being afraid of something can be thought of as a syndrome of symptoms: in a particular case, certain symptoms may be particularly pronounced while other symptoms may be slight or even missing altogether.[8] "'Grief' describes a pattern which recurs, with dif-

6. The passage from Darwin's *Origin of the Emotions* is quoted in James's *The Principles of Psychology,* II (New York: Holt, 1890), 446–447.

7. *Op. cit.,* II, 451. The emphasis is James's.

8. This idea is developed by Anthony Kenny in *Action, Emotion, and Will* (London: Routledge & Kegan Paul, 1963), pp. 67–70.

ferent variations, in the weave of our life. If a man's bodily expression of sorrow and of joy alternated, say with the ticking of a clock, here we should not have the characteristic formation of the pattern of sorrow or the pattern of joy."⁹

Fear, too, is "a pattern which recurs, with different variations, in the weave of our life." Someone who believes that pain and injury are the worst calamity that can befall him and that nothing is worth risking them, so that he avoids such risks at all costs, is afraid of being injured. He is more afraid of being injured than most. Since this effectively incapacitates him for normal activity, he is excessively afraid. One might also say of this person that he is mistaken, that he is ignorant of what is most important and worth while. This assertion, however, is not incompatible with saying that his practical reasoning is faulty due to his being excessively afraid of injury.

Since fear admits of variations in this way, it is not surprising that fear can undermine practical reasoning in more than one way: it can lead (force, drive) one to do what one knows one should not do, but it can also corrupt the reasoning process itself, so that the agent comes to think that he should do something that he should not do. Thus, condition (iv) takes the form of a disjunction of a pair of conditions, each one corresponding to a way in which fear disrupts practical reasoning. Sometimes we are confident that a certain action is cowardly, that it satisfies one or the other of the two disjuncts in (iv), but we are not clear *which* of these two conditions is satisfied. Sometimes the agent himself does not know. In the passage from *Lord Jim* cited at the beginning of this chapter, Jim hesitated while his fellows manned and launched a rescue boat. This is a small incident, and we are not told what he thought. It could be, though, that Jim himself could tell us no more. Fear lay behind his hesitation, but it is not clear how it operated. This sort of ambiguity, and the attendant conceptual flexibility, is one of the factors which makes it possible to

9. Ludwig Wittgenstein, *Philosophical Investigations*, trans. G. E. M. Anscombe (New York: Macmillan, 1953), p. 174e.

defend with some plausibility a negative answer to the question, 'Does a person ever voluntarily take what he believes to be the greater of two evils or the lesser of two goods?'

Conditions (i)–(iv) are intended to be necessary conditions for a cowardly act. Are they jointly sufficient? Since the first disjunct in (iv) simply states that the agent does not have a certain belief, it appears that all four conditions might be satisfied in a case in which A is undecided about whether the risk involved in doing Y is worth the benefits. It is doubtful that in *all* such cases, A's doing X rather than Y would be cowardly. People sometimes find themselves in complex and unusual situations where they must act quickly. In confusion and doubt, A might do X rather than Y because he fears the risks involved in doing Y, and he might have no idea whether he should do X or not. If A's doubts and fears result from his being *excessively* afraid, that is, if but for his excessive fear, A would have seen that doing Y is worth the risks, then A's doing X is cowardly. On the other hand, if A panics because of terrible danger, and his fear is not excessive, then his doing X because he is afraid to do Y may not be cowardly. "There are things terrible even beyond human strength. These, then, are terrible to everyone—at least to every sensible man. . . " (*NE* 1115b7–8). It is possible to reformulate (iv) in such a way that cases in which A is prevented by a not-excessive fear from deciding whether doing Y is worth the risks can no longer satisfy this condition:

(iv′) *Either*

A believes that his doing Y would be worth the risks it involves

Or

If A does not believe this, his not believing this is due to his being *excessively* afraid of the risks of doing Y.

Conditions (i)–(iii) and (iv′) are necessary conditions for A's doing X to be cowardly, but there are at least two sorts of circumstances in which all four conditions might be satisfied, yet A's act not be cowardly. The first sort of circumstance is that described by Aristotle—the dangers of doing Y are "terrible beyond human strength," yet A believes that his doing Y would be worth the risks. If we view cowardice as something that incapacitates a person for normal activity in a world that presents certain kinds and degrees of dangers in the normal course of things, then it is not surprising that being unable to cope with extraordinary dangers of a degree far exceeding what is normally encountered is not characteristic of cowardice.

A second sort of circumstance in which the four conditions might be satisfied but the act not be cowardly is this: Although A thinks that doing Y is worth the risks it involves, really it would be foolish for A to do Y and face such risks. If A were to try to do Y but fail because he is afraid, it is not clear that his doing X rather than Y is cowardly. Suppose, for example, that A wants to show off by playing a round of Russian roulette, but when he has pointed the gun at himself, he is afraid to pull the trigger. It is not surprising that this sort of behavior is not regarded as cowardly, since here, rather than distorting his practical reasoning or preventing him from acting upon sound decisions, A's fear saves him from folly.

We can set down conditions for an act's being cowardly that will hold for the most part. At the same time, however, we must understand our interest in cowardice and understand the role it plays in our lives. When such conditions are satisfied in circumstances in which there is a reversal of the phenomenon's usual role, then we may not regard the action as cowardly. In the Russian roulette example, the usual marks of a cowardly act are there, yet the upshot in this case is that reason is served and folly averted. A similar point might be made about philosophical accounts of many different things. Generally, however, barring cases in which the risks of doing Y are so terrible that no one could be expected to face them, and barring cases in which it would be foolhardy for A to do Y, if conditions (i)–(iv') are satisfied, then A's doing X will be fully characteristic of cowardice.

A coward, then, is someone whose excessive fears prevent him from acting upon his practical reasoning in situations in which it would be neither foolhardy nor beyond human endurance to do so, or whose excessive fears lead him in his practical reasoning to give too much weight to dangers, with the result that he avoids actions he would otherwise do. A person's cowardice might be limited to certain sorts of dangers—he might, for example, be excessively afraid of physical injury, but not of censure, disapproval, or loss of economic security. A coward, however, is someone who is incapacitated.

3. *Courage*

The sort of courage that concerns us here is the virtue that corresponds to the vice cowardice. It is the opposite of cowardice, the ability to weigh up correctly the pros and cons of various alternative courses of action when some courses involve danger and the ability to face dangers. Courage and bravery are sometimes ascribed to individuals who bear up under grief and adversity, but we would not, I think, call someone a *coward* because he went to pieces in such circumstances. An exception to this statement is to be found in situations that confront a person with a fearful evil he can in no way avoid. A person shows courage in facing his certain death with dignity and composure, whereas one who gibbers with fear might be thought to be cowardly. The kind of courage that is concerned with the facing of dangers where one has a choice in the matter generally involves the ability to master fear. This same fear-mastering ability is apt to be required to face certain death with composure. One whose fear overcame him in the face of certain death might be presumed to lack the ability to face danger in situations in which he might avoid the danger. The kind of courage that is most important and most useful, however, has to do with facing dangers where one has a choice in the matter. I will discuss this kind of courage.

Every courageous act must have some aim or end that the agent has reason to regard as important or worth while. Simply the fact that an act is a brave act, however, provides no clue as to the aim of the act or to the agent's motive. Some virtues are such that the acts fully characteristic of them must be done from a certain motive—for example, honesty and generosity. To be told that a certain act is fully characteristic of the virtue generosity is to be given some idea of the purpose or motive behind it, and sometimes no further explanation of the act is necessary. An example would be giving one's coat to a beggar on a generous impulse. People do not in the same way do things simply upon the prompting of courage. Courage, in this respect, is not a motive. Courage is a virtue that is shown in acting for other ends and goals, but it is not itself a motive in the way that honesty, kindness, and generosity are. One might do something in order to demonstrate one's bravery, but this does not make bravery a motive. Consider the fact that someone might do something in order to demonstrate his generosity. It does not follow from this that his *motive* in doing this is generosity. In fact, it is hard to see how generosity could be his motive in such a case. Questions like 'Why do that?' 'What is the point of doing that?' and 'What is his motive in doing that?' are not answered by pointing out that the act in question is brave. These points confirm the claim made at the outset that from the standpoint of the motivational view of character traits, courage is a privative state. Cowardice is a tendency to be motivated by fear in certain ways, and courage, rather than being a tendency to be motivated in a particular way, is the absence of this tendency characteristic of cowardice. On the other hand, one can also regard courage as the positive ability to cope rationally with fears and to face dangers.

Being kind or generous involves being likely to act from a certain sort of motive— wanting to help people and being willing to put oneself out to do this. Being brave, on the other hand, does not seem to involve acting from any particular sort of motive or for any particular ends. Consequently, one can act from motives that are morally reprehensible and still show courage. Protagoras, in Plato's dialogue by that name, may be right when he maintains that one could possess courage and none of the other virtues. Why could not a person be totally corrupt and insensitive and at the same time be brave?

Courage is sometimes classified as a "self-regarding" virtue, as opposed to an "other-regarding" virtue, on the grounds that courage, like prudence, serves primarily the good of the courageous person himself. This view is misleading, however. Kind and generous acts are necessarily intended to benefit another, and courageous acts are not *necessarily* so intended. When, however, the good of others or the common good is or should be the decisive consideration in what one does, courage might very well serve the well-being of others. It is because a courageous person can be counted upon when the common good is threatened that courage is so prized. Prudence is essentially a virtue that concerns one's own crucial interests, and kindness is essentially concerned with others' good. Courage, like patience and industry, could serve the interests of the agent himself, but also the interests of others.

Since courage is the opposite of cowardice, there will be conditions for courageous acts that are the counterparts of the conditions for cowardly acts. Let us suppose that A does Y, and the following conditions are satisfied.

(a)   A believes that it is dangerous for him to do Y.

(b)   A believes that his doing Y is worth the risks it involves.

(c)   A believes that it is possible for him not to do Y.

Condition (a) is a necessary condition for A's doing Y being a courageous act. Someone who sees no peril in what he does is not acting courageously. The danger involved may be danger of injury or death for A or it may be danger of economic loss, loss of prestige, ostracism, or censure. Danger, here, is anything that threatens A's well-being. If (a) obtains, and A does Y, then A's action would be foolish or reckless if (b) were not true. Condition (c) requires that A think that he has some choice in the matter. When an army is aware that deep trenches have been dug behind them so that they cannot retreat, then they are not being courageous when they stand their ground under attack.

Conditions (a), (b), and (c), however, are not jointly sufficient for A's doing Y to be courageous. Where the danger is slight and the reward substantial, doing Y will not necessarily be courageous. There is danger involved in automobile travel, but people are not being courageous when they drive their cars. This suggests that the danger involved must be great enough so that it is difficult to do the act in question—not necessarily difficult for the agent, but at least difficult for most people. Aristotle says in the *Eudemian Ethics:*

> What, then, a coward as such fears is not formidable to any one or but slightly so; but what is formidable to the majority of men or to human nature, that we call absolutely formidable. But the brave man shows himself fearless towards these and endures such things, they being to him formidable in one sense but in another not—formidable to him *qua* man, but not formidable to him except slightly so, or not at all, *qua* brave. These things, however, are terrible, for they are so to the majority of men.[10]

This suggests still another necessary condition for a courageous act.

(d) The danger A sees in doing Y must be sufficiently formidable that most people would find it difficult in the circumstances to do Y.

Some acts are more courageous than others, and how courageous an act is depends upon how difficult it would be for us to face the danger the act is supposed by the agent to involve.

Sometimes, however, when a person faces a danger of which he is terribly afraid, but that other people would not find formidable, we do see courage involved in his act even though condition (d) is not satisfied. He shows ability to master great fear, which is one of the capacities involved in courage, but his fear of the situation is excessive. The latter suggests that if the danger were increased a bit, then he would be too afraid to do Y, and his not doing Y would be likely to be cowardly. The two aspects of courage and cowardice—the "Kantian" or fear-mastering aspect and the matter of having the appropriate degree of fear—conflict in such a case, and it is not surprising that we are pulled in two directions on the question of whether such acts are courageous. One might say in such a case that doing Y is brave *for the agent*, but it would not be correct to say unqualifiedly that his doing Y is courageous.

10. 1228b24–30. The translation is by J. Solomon in W. D. Ross, ed., *The Works of Aristotle*, Vol. IX (Oxford, 1915).

An agent, in performing a courageous act, need not feel any fear at all, nor need he feel the act difficult. We admire the courage of someone who does something very dangerous so coolly that it appears to be easy for him. It is necessary, however, in order for his act to be courageous, that he be aware of the danger and that he recognize it as a danger.

If conditions (a), (b), (c), and (d) are fulfilled, and the agent is *coerced* into doing Y, his doing Y may not be courageous. Aristotle remarks that soldiers who go into battle because they are threatened with terrible punishments if they refuse show an inferior kind of courage. "One ought to be brave not under compulsion but because it is noble to be so" (1116b2–3). These are cases in which a person faces danger because his only alternative is to face a different danger that he fears more. Now if a soldier's fear of fighting is excessive to begin with, so that he will not fight unless he is forced to do so, it is not surprising that his fighting under compulsion is not regarded as courageous. If one does Y because one is coerced by threats of terrible punishments if one does not do Y, then even though conditions (a)–(d) are satisfied, one's doing Y will not be courageous.

Apparently similar to the case of the soldier who fights because he fears punishment if he refuses is the following: A soldier fights because of his fear of being a coward, his fear of reproach both from others and from himself. Suppose that he would not fight but for his horror of being cowardly. It seems clear that his fighting may well be brave. Why should fear of punishment disqualify an act from being brave, while fear of cowardice does not? There is this difference between the two cases: the second case, unlike the first, does not involve coercion. Why should this make any difference? A person who regards cowardly acts as shameful will thereby quite generally and systematically be strengthened for the dictates of reason in the face of danger. Someone might be brave without regarding cowardice as shameful, but the view that cowardice is shameful and the strong desire to avoid it clearly reinforce the effect of courage.

Another condition, then, for A's doing Y to be courageous rules out his being compelled by fear of punishment to do Y.

(e)   A is not coerced into doing Y by threats of punishment,
        which he fears more than he fears the dangers of doing Y.

There is at least one other condition necessary for an act's
being courageous. We do not see courage exemplified in the acts
of individuals who, because of frenzy, stupor, or intoxication, are
not in control of themselves. Since courage is concerned with
practical reasoning in the face of danger and acting upon the
results of that reasoning, it is not surprising that we do not see
courage in the behavior of someone whose powers of reasoning
and apprehension are not functioning—someone who does not
fully know what he is doing or who is not in control of himself.

The concepts of cowardice and courage, then, encapsulate the
following suppositions. First, fear can prevent a person from
doing what he thinks is best. Second, fear can lead a person to
give too much weight to dangers in deciding what course of
action is best. In this way, fear can disrupt one's practical reasoning, and it can prevent one from acting on the result of one's
practical reasoning. When a person is such that in certain kinds
of common situations, fear either distorts his practical reasoning
so that he decides against dangerous courses of action that he
would otherwise adopt, or fear prevents him from doing dangerous acts when he thinks these acts are best, then he suffers an
incapacity. That is, there are things people normally can do that
such a person is barred from doing. In this respect, a coward is
like a person who is injured or ill. Some people, on the other
hand, have the ability to weigh courses of action involving danger
without giving too much weight to the danger, and even to adopt
courses of action involving danger in situations where the danger
is so great that most people would have difficulty in managing
their fear. Such people are courageous. The function of courage,
then, is to preserve practical reasoning and enable it to issue in
action in the face of danger.

4. Self-Indulgence

Like cowardice, self-indulgence is a vice that consists in a
tendency to be influenced excessively by a certain sort of motive
or consideration. Aristotle classified courage and *sōphrosunē* to-

gether on the grounds that these are "virtues of the irrational parts" (*NE* III, 10, 1117b22–23), and this classification suggests that both have to do with desires that are particularly apt to oppose reason. Cowardice, however, has to do with the emotion, fear, whereas self-indulgence is not similarly related to a particular emotion. This makes a difference, because fear sometimes can *force* or *drive* a person to do something, whereas someone who succumbs to self-indulgence yields to temptations. Characteristically, he is seduced rather than driven. This, perhaps, is what Aristotle had in mind when he said, "Self-indulgence is more like a voluntary state than cowardice" (*NE* III, 12, 1119a22–23). One cannot *coerce* or *force* a person to do something by promising to reward him for doing it. Coercion involves the threat of pain or harm. Similarly, the prospect of pleasure or amusement may be said to *induce* someone to act, but not *force* him to act.

A self-indulgent person is one who indulges himself—of course—more than he should, in certain sorts of pleasures and amusements. Aristotle said that the *akolastos*, the self-indulgent man, is excessively fond of pleasures involving touch, particularly eating, drinking, and sexual intercourse. According to Sir David Ross, '*akolasia*' was originally applied by the Greeks to "the ways of small children"—undisciplined children. Aristotle remarked on the aptness of the transference of this word from undisciplined children to adults who live at the beck and call of their appetites.[11] Much is made in Aristotle's account of the fact that the *akolastos* occupies himself excessively with things that, because they are enjoyed by animals, appear "slavish and brutish."

The English word, "self-indulgence," does not have the connotations of undisciplined childishness of "*akolasia*." The two notions are concerned with the same sorts of pleasures, however, and the analogy with a certain sort of childishness is illuminating. It is important to notice that not just any preoccupation with

11. *Nicomachean Ethics* 1119a34–b20. See also W. D. Ross's footnote to this passage in *The Works of Aristotle*, Vol. IX.

food, drink, or sex is characteristic of self-indulgence. When a person exerts considerable effort and energy to gratify his appetites, we are not apt to see self-indulgence behind what he does. In Choderlos de Laclos's novel *Les Liaisons dangereuses*, for example, Madame de Merteuil and Valmont are occupied continually with seductions and sexual conquests. Their intrigues are so complicated and their campaigns so protracted and strenuous, however, that even if we suppose that their main aim is sexual pleasure, they seem not at all self-indulgent. They demonstrate fortitude, restraint and perseverance—all qualities contrary to self-indulgence. Self-indulgence has to do with *easy* pleasures and amusements—ones that require no particular effort or sacrifice to secure and enjoy. One who devotes himself to seeking pleasure by complex or difficult means is not self-indulgent.

Epicurus held that the best human life would consist in pleasure and the absence of pain, but the sort of life he thought most conducive to this is very different from the life of the self-indulgent individual.

And since pleasure is the first good and natural to us, for this very reason we do not choose every pleasure, but sometimes we pass over many pleasures, when greater discomfort accrues to us as a result of them. . . .

When, therefore, we maintain that pleasure is the end, we do not mean the pleasures of profligates and those that consist in sensuality. . . . For it is not continuous drinkings and revelings nor the satisfaction of lusts . . . which produce a pleasant life, but sober reasoning, searching out the motives for all choice and avoidance, and banishing mere opinions. . . .

Of all this the beginning and the greatest good is prudence [*phronēsis*[.[12]

A self-indulgent person does pursue simple, easily accessible pleasures and amusements. Often, these are pleasures that children and animals also enjoy. The activity characteristic of self-indulgence is apt to be unstructured and unplanned. It is to be contrasted with the behavior of someone who takes part in a

---

12. "Letter to Menoeceus," in Cyril Bailey, ed. and trans., *Epicurus* (Oxford: Clarendon Press, 1926), pp. 87–91.

prolonged, difficult, or arduous enterprise in which the goal is at some distance from the starting point. Characteristically, the self-indulgent person is unwilling or unable to forego an immediate pleasure when considerations indicate that he should.

Are there conditions for an act's being fully characteristic of self-indulgence analogous to the conditions for a cowardly act, (i)–(iv′)? We do not apply the adjective 'self-indulgent' to particular acts as often as we do the adjective 'cowardly.' Moreover, self-indulgence typically exhibits itself in a pattern of activity over time. Individual actions that are clearly a part of such a pattern may lose their connection with self-indulgence when they are taken out of the pattern. Watching a football game on television is not by itself evidence of self-indulgence. Watching *every* football game televised—five or six games a week during the season—instead of getting needed exercise may evidence self-indulgence.

This, however, does not show that particular acts are never fully characteristic of self-indulgence. Of course, if there is no reason why one should not watch an occasional football game, then single instances of such behavior are not apt to exhibit self-indulgence. A pattern, in which this and other easy pleasures are repeated until there is some harm or fault in it, will be characteristic of self-indulgence. *Excessive* fondness for easy pleasures and amusement is apt to be exhibited by doing things many people find enjoyable, but doing these things more often or at greater cost, until some harm is done. Excessive fear, on the other hand, is more apt to be exhibited in particular actions that show forth the excessive fear in the particular action. If, however, on a particular occasion, there is something one should do, and one chooses instead some amusement that lies at hand, then this particular act may, by itself, be fully characteristic of self-indulgence. If there are such acts, then the proper account of what it is for an act to be fully characteristic of self-indulgence may well be analogous to the account of cowardly acts.

The following is, I think, a clear example of a particular act fully characteristic of self-indulgence. In his account of Hitler's

Ardennes counterstroke in December 1944, the military historian B. H. Liddell Hart says: "On the 18th, the Germans came close to Bastogne—after an advance of nearly thirty miles, but their attempt to rush this key road-centre on the 19th was checked." In a footnote, Liddell Hart adds: "Not entirely by the defenders—for a spearhead commander confessed to me in later discussion that at this vital moment he dallied with a young American nurse, 'blonde and beautiful', who held him spellbound in a village his troops had overrun. Battles are not always decided in the way that the military textbooks teach!"[13]

Following the model of the account of cowardly acts given, we might begin in the following way. In order for A's doing X to be fully characteristic of self-indulgence, there must be some action Y such that:

(1) A is doing X rather than Y.
(2) A believes that he has some reason to do Y.
(3) A is doing X rather than Y because doing X is pleasant or amusing.

These three conditions, of course, are counterparts of conditions (i)–(iii) for a cowardly act. If the accounts of self-indulgence and cowardice are to correspond closely, there will be a fourth condition for an act of self-indulgence, a condition that concerns the relation of practical reason to A's desire to do X rather than Y. One possibility is that A knows perfectly well that he should do Y, but doing X is so attractive, so tempting, that he yields. This, no doubt, is how it was with the tank commander with a weakness for blond tresses. Perhaps he was so entranced that he forgot for a while what he was supposed to do, but there can be no doubt that he knew. If, however, there is to be a fourth condition here analogous to condition (iv') for a cowardly act, this condition (4) will be a disjunction. One disjunct will be:

(4.1) A believes that all things considered, he should do Y rather than X.

In the account of cowardly acts, the second disjunct of (iv')

13. *History of the Second World War* (New York: Putnam's, 1971), p. 651.

allows for the possibility that the agent's excessive fear leads him to give too much weight to danger, so that there is no opposition between what *he* thinks he should do and what fear inclines him to do. Is there an analogous possibility with acts of self-indulgence? Could someone's excessive fondness for certain pleasures and amusements lead him to give too much weight to these things in his practical reasoning so that he acts in ways *fully* characteristic of self-indulgence?

Aristotle clearly thought so. He distinguished between *akrasia* (weakness of will) and *akolasia* (self-indulgence). He would have regarded an act that satisfies (1)–(4.1) as characteristic of *akrasia* rather than *akolasia*. The *akratēs* (weak man), Aristotle said, "is like a city which passes all the right decrees and has good laws, but makes no use of them," while the *akolastos* "is like a city that uses its laws, but has wicked laws to use" (*NE* VII, 10, 1152a20–24). On this account, a self-indulgent person would be one who thought he should avail himself of his favorite pleasures and amusements at every opportunity.

Our concept of self-indulgence, unlike Aristotle's, includes weakness of will with respect to pleasures and amusements. The question is whether it also applies to the individual who holds that pleasures and amusements are the most important things in life, *and* who acts as a self-indulgent person would act, believing that this is what he should do. This, of course, is Aristotle's *akolastos*.

Can there be *principled* self-indulgence? Given the nature of human beings and the conditions of human life, it is difficult to see how anyone of normal intelligence and experience who had given the matter any thought at all could hold principles that would lead him to act *always* as a self-indulgent person would act. For example, were a self-indulgent glutton to try to rationalize his behavior, to show that he is following a coherent plan for living as well as he can, he would quickly find himself in an untenable position. His view of a good life is to get as much gustatory pleasure as possible, and he must consider how best to do this. Insuring himself of a continuing supply of food is apt to require considerable effort. Moreover, excessive eating will ruin his health, spoil his enjoyment, and shorten his life. A reasonable person planning a life of gustatory pleasure must take such things into account and admit the desirability of a certain degree of restraint. Such restraint, however, is uncharacteristic of a self-indulgent person. Pleasures obtained at the price of restraint cease by that fact to be altogether easy pleasures. Self-indulgence and restraint are *contrary* traits.

To be able successfully to follow *any* life plan, including a bad one, one will invariably need a certain degree of temperance and restraint. This is the function of such virtues. They are required because of the way the world is. The notion of *principled* self-indulgence, therefore, is curiously at odds with itself. A self-indulgent person might convince himself that some sort of rationale covered his self-indulgent behavior, but only by not looking closely at the matter or by self-deception. A person who seriously tries to rationalize his hedonism will find himself drawn in the direction of Epicurus, at least to the extent of being forced to admit that restraint is a virtue.

The paradigm of a self-indulgent individual, then, is not someone consistently following a coherent but mistaken life-plan. He is not like a city that adheres to a bad set of laws. In defense of Aristotle, one might insist that the consummately self-indulgent person does have a plan. His policy is to pursue any pleasure or amusement that is easily obtainable—whatever lies at hand. To adopt Aristotle's own analogy, however, such a person is like a city that solemnly enacts the law "Do as you please." In both cases, one may surround these pronouncements with all the ceremonial trappings of plans and laws, but the performance is a sham. In effect, they are equivalent to having no plan or law. They are, if you like, degenerate cases of plans and laws, as a point is a degenerate case of a circle.

There are then at least two sorts of "ideal"—that is, paradigmatic—self-indulgent individuals. One is weak and abandons his plans when he can pursue easy pleasures and amusements. The other pursues easy pleasures without any reservations, because he has no plans to abandon. Real people who are more or less self-indulgent conform more or less to one or the other of these paradigms, often with an overlay of rationalization and self-deception that disguises their weakness or planlessness. Self-indulgence is an incapacity, then, in a way comparable to the incapacity of a coward. A self-indulgent individual is limited in the sort of life he can lead. His difficulty is that, at least at times, he lacks the direction of a plan, either because, like a child, he has no real plan, or, if he has one, he fails to follow it when pleasures and amusements beckon.

Human life consists, in large measure, in following plans. It may be that many people do not have a worked-out life-plan that they can articulate in much detail, but this does not mean that they lack plans. Most of our plans are given to us. The mode of life characteristic of human beings is a social life in communities, a life structured by many highly complex social institutions and conventions. Life for an individual in a community involves playing myriad roles created and drawn by these conventions. These institutions present individuals with plans. This, of course, is not at all simple, because the multiplicity of an individual's roles engenders conflicts that he must resolve. An individual is in this way presented with goals and pathways to them, but also with problems and conflicts that are obstacles. A person must chart his path through these obstacles, together, of course, with whatever other difficulties the world presents. To resolve such conflicts and to solve such problems intelligently is to deal creatively with the framework of conventions and institutions. Such a life represents the work of practical reason. To choose to act reasonably, Dewey said, is to choose to act "with regard to the claims of each of the competing habits and impulses." The basis for such "claims" must be sought in the complex of insitutions that structure human life. To the extent that an individual is self-indulgent, he is handicapped in leading such a life.

A fourth condition for A's doing X to be fully characteristic of self-indulgence, a condition modeled upon condition (iv′) for a cowardly act would be:

(4)   *Either*

    (4.1) A really believes that all things considered, he should do Y rather than X.

Or

(4.2) If A does not believe this, his not believing this is
due to his being excessively fond of easy pleasures
and amusements.

The second disjunct, (4.2), must be understood in conjunction
with the discussion that precedes it. There is a distinction, a
contrast, to be drawn between self-indulgence and a carefully
worked out hedonism that requires restraint for its execution.
The self-indulgent person is excessively fond of *easy* pleasures,
and it is the propinquity as much as the pleasantness that excessively influences him. He ignores Sidgwick's principle which
says, in one memorable formulation, "Hereafter *as such* is to be
regarded neither less nor more than Now."[14] This attitude
gives the self-indulgent person's activity the dimension of planlessness and incapacitates him for a life that is characteristically
one of planned activity.

It is truly said, then, that the function of courage and restraint
(*sōphrosunē*) is the preservation of practical reason. Both knowing
what one should do and acting upon one's knowledge are difficult
when there are dangers to be faced or temptations to be resisted.
One may see this difficulty as an opposition between reason and
passion. Acts fully characteristic of cowardice or self-indulgence,
however, are not always the result of the agent's losing a struggle
with fear or temptation, although they sometimes are. It may be
simply that the agent gives too much weight to dangers in his
practical reasoning or that he is too much influenced by the
prospect of easy gratification. Both dangers and pleasures cause
various problems for human beings, and the functions of courage
and *sōphrosunē* can be understood by reference to these problems.

14. Henry Sidgwick, *The Methods of Ethics*, 7th ed. (Chicago: University of
Chicago Press, 1962), p. 381.

IV

Conscientiousness

Traits of character that focus in a certain way upon the observance of forms of behavior I call forms of conscientiousness. Among these traits are honesty, fairness, truthfulness, and being a person of one's word. Kindness and generosity, which are forms of benevolence rather than conscientiousness, involve a concern for other people. This concern is, in an important respect, like the attitude of lovers and friends toward one another. The feelings and actions that accompany these virtues are often very satisfying to the agent himself and very congenial to other people. Honesty, truthfulness, fairness, and being a person of one's word, by contrast, are commitments to forms of behavior rather than concerns for the happiness, security, and comfort of other people. The attitudes characteristic of honesty, for example, are quite different from the attitudes characteristic of affection and friendship. Such traits as truthfulness and honesty do not make a person likeable in the way that kindness and generosity do. The former traits do not engage our affections—they are not, in Hume's words, "amiable virtues."

"Conscientiousness" here is a technical term. Actions fully characteristic of virtues that are forms of conscientiousness are the sort that moral philosophers regard as manifesting a sense of duty or obligation. The word has a somewhat different meaning in common speech where it is used more broadly than in my use and carries connotations of meticulousness and attention to detail. There is considerable precedent in the philosophical literature, however, for this technical use of the term.

A man might have a direct pro-attitude towards obeying a moral rule or towards doing what he thinks his duty, as such; he may have no desire whatever to do the action apart from its being his duty and no thought of the consequences, for himself or others, that the action is likely to produce. Now this motive is exactly what we mean by the Sense of Duty and the man who acts on it is called conscientious.[1]

A person who is conscientious about behaving in a certain way is, I shall say, "intrinsically motivated" to act in that way. That is, so acting is itself one of his aims, quite apart from the consequences of so acting. Thus, being conscientious about a certain form of action involves being intrinsically motivated as opposed to being instrumentally motivated so to act. Such a person, as Nowell-Smith says, may have no desire "to do the action apart from its being his duty and no thought of its consequences."

This suggests that the attitude of someone who is conscientious about, say, avoiding cheating is like a skiing enthusiast's attitude toward skiing. Each would be disposed to engage in his action even if so doing did not produce anything else he wants. Of course, there is an obvious and striking difference between the attitudes toward their respective actions of the skiing enthusiast and the conscientious person. A skiing enthusiast likes to ski, but he will never for that reason feel that he has to ski whether he wants to or not. A person who is conscientious about avoiding cheating, however, characteristically does feel that he must avoid cheating whether he wants to or not. He might contemplate cheating if it were clearly the lesser of two evils, but otherwise he regards an inclination to cheat as something to be resisted. He regards cheating as wrong.

1. P. H. Nowell-Smith, *Ethics* (Harmondsworth, Middlesex: Penguin Books, 1954), p. 245.

It is as though a conscientious person sees himself as bound by rules or laws that he is required to obey. This model is, for good reasons, pervasive in moral philosophy. Difficulties arise, however, when we ask what the incentive is to obey such laws. Rewards or punishments extrinsic to the action prescribed cannot be the conscientious person's incentive, since he is intrinsically motivated. This point is argued vigorously by Kant. Yet the idea that we have to do what is prescribed by certain rules, with no incentive apart from the nature of the acts themselves or the fact that they are prescribed, is puzzling. The difficulty does not disappear if the rule model is abandoned. The puzzle appears to originate with the phenomenon of conscientiousness itself—someone's conviction that he has to behave in a certain way, joined with his being intrinsically motivated to act in that way.

What I am calling "conscientiousness" is a common phenomenon. It is conceived by some people as having to do somehow with religion, by others as having to do with tradition, or benevolence, or the nature of reason itself. These conceptions are not always consistent or coherent. Not every sort of conscientiousness is praiseworthy. Some human excellences, however—honesty, truthfulness, fairness, and being a person of one's word, for example—are forms of conscientiousness, or so I shall maintain. These virtues, so conceived, have indispensable functions in our lives, which could not be fulfilled by virtues that are not forms of conscientiousness. I shall argue, too, that these virtues perform certain of their functions better than would other forms of conscientiousness that might be called conscientious altruism or benevolence.

Connected with the difficulty of understanding how someone can at the same time regard an action as necessary *and* be intrinsically motivated to do it is the question of how a person who is conscientious about a certain form of behavior can regard his attitude as reasonable. Also, how can a conscientious person be reasonable in reaching decisions where there is a conflict of obligations or where other serious considerations oppose his conscientiousness? It is not easy to see how he can, and this is at least one reason why some regard conscientiousness as a primitive stage of moral development or a second-best sort of virtue for those whose growth in heart and mind is stunted. Charles Dickens' description in *Bleak House* of Sir Leicester Dedlock sketches this type.

He would on the whole admit Nature to be a good idea (a little low, perhaps, when not enclosed with a park-fence), but an idea dependent for its execution on your great country families. He is a gentleman of strict conscience, disdainful of all littleness and meanness, and ready, on the shortest notice, to die any death you may please to mention rather than give occasion for the least impeachment of his integrity. He is an honourable, obstinate, truthful, high-spirited, intensely prejudiced, perfectly unreasonable man.

Conscientiousness, of course, is not a substitute for intelligence, imagination, and good judgment. Not only is there no incompatibility between possessing virtues that are forms of conscientiousness and being reasonable and humane, however, but the possession of all these things is absolutely necessary for moral sensitivity and good judgment.

1. Prichard's Problem

The intuitionist moral philosopher, Harold A. Prichard, in his account of what he called the "sense of obligation," posed in a particularly striking way the problem of how a conscientious person can regard himself as reasonable in his conscientiousness. In his famous article "Does Moral Philosophy Rest on a Mistake?" Prichard argued that attempts to show that we should do what is called "our duty" cannot succeed, and justification of our belief that we should do such things is neither possible nor necessary.[2] To the question 'Why should one do what is normally called

2. H. A. Prichard, *Moral Obligation* (Oxford: Clarendon Press, 1949), pp. 1–17. Numbers in parentheses in the text refer to pages in his book. This article originally appeared in *Mind*, 21, no. 81 (1912).

"one's duty"?' there are only two possible sorts of answers, according to Prichard. He maintains that both sorts of answers are unsatisfactory (2).

One sort of answer to this question consists in showing that doing one's duty is itself something one wants to do or that it leads to something one wants. This answer, Prichard argues, may make one want to do these things, but it does not show that one is obligated to do them (2–3). The other sort of answer is "an answer which bases the obligation to do something on the *goodness* either of something to which the act leads or of the act itself" (3). Prichard finds these answers unsatisfactory, because even if these actions are good or lead to something good, it would not follow that one is *obligated* to do them (3–4). Moreover, Prichard maintains, if we consider carefully why we feel obligated to be truthful, pay our debts, etc., we will see that this does not rest on our recognition that in every case such acts will produce something good (4–5). Such acts are, of course, themselves good, but their goodness *as conscientious acts* depends upon their being done because the agent feels obligated to do them. Thus, the agent does not first see the intrinsic goodness of such actions and subsequently conclude that he is obligated to do them (5–7).[3]

The question 'Why should one do what is normally called "one's duty"?' is improper, Prichard contends, because once one has seen the nature of such acts, that one ought to do them is self-evident and underivative (7–8).

I wish to phrase in this way the question with which Prichard struggled: How can someone be intrinsically motivated to act in a certain way and at the same time *reasonably* feel that he *has to* act in that way? What sorts of reasons or justifications can one give for one's regarding such a mode of behavior as being truthful or paying one's debts in both of these ways at once? The sorts of

3. Prichard also considers the possibility that the action gets its goodness from an intrinsically good motive such as gratitude, affection, or public spirit. He rejects this possibility on the grounds that such a motive does not give rise to "the sense of obligation to do it" (6).

reasons that one might offer for being intrinsically motivated to act in a certain way (e.g., one likes doing it, it is interesting to do, it is good in some way) do not account for one's feeling that one *has to* act in this way. The sort of reason one might give for thinking that one has to do something—that it is necessary for something else—seems ruled out by the fact that the action is intrinsically motivated. Conscientious actions have two aspects—they are (1) intrinsically motivated and (2) necessary. It appears that whatever reason one might give for one aspect will clash with the other aspect. Prichard falls back upon the claim that the obligatoriness of such actions is "self-evident." Thus, were someone to ask what grounds an honest person has for thinking that he should avoid cheating, Prichard's answer is, "None—but he doesn't need any." For some purposes, this answer might be perfectly satisfactory. If one wants to understand conscientiousness, however, and if one wants to know why it is reasonable to be conscientious about some actions and not others, this answer is disappointing. The appeal to self-evidence does not contribute to our understanding of conscientiousness. Moreover, it leaves us with no way of dealing with disagreements about what is self-evident, no way of assuring ourselves that the self-evidence of something is more than apparent.

Leaving aside the epistemological doctrine of the self-evidence of certain duties, Prichard has given an accurate description of the beliefs and attitudes of many people who are honest, fair, persons of their word, and truthful. Individuals who are both conscientious and philosophically reflective may have a variety of more complicated beliefs about these matters, but Prichard has described the core phenomenon.

We are confronted with the problem Prichard posed: how can we be intrinsically motivated to act in certain ways and at the same time reasonably feel that we ought to act in those ways? In the following sections, I will explore some aspects of virtues that are forms of conscientiousness in search of ways of dealing with Prichard's problem.

2. *Hobbes Situations*

Most people have in some degree at least some of the virtues that are forms of conscientiousness. These traits are valued for a number of reasons, and they have several functions in human life. To develop this thesis I will use two familiar ideas about morality. One of these ideas derives from Hobbes's political philosophy. It has been formulated recently in a particularly striking way by David Gauthier.[4]

There is a kind of situation involving two or more people that I will call a Hobbes situation. A Hobbes situation is one in which there is a certain mode of behavior, B, of which all of the following are true.

(1) Everyone is apt to benefit if all or most people in the situation conform to B, but this benefit is not realized unless most conform.

(2) Conforming to B generally involves some sacrifice, so that, other things being equal, it is apt to be maximally advantageous for an individual not to conform when most conform.

(3) As a rule, the sacrifice involved for an individual in conforming to B is small in comparison with the benefit to him of the conformity of most people to B.

(4) It is apt to be maximally disadvantageous to an individual to conform to B when not enough others conform to realize the benefit.

The most interesting thing about such situations is that, from the standpoint of his own advantage, an individual will do better *not* to conform to B no matter what other people do. If enough people in the situation realize this and try to do as well for themselves as possible, there will not be enough conformity to B to realize the benefit, and everyone loses. Thus considerations of

4. "Morality and Advantage," *Philosophical Review*, 76 (1967), 460–475. My discussion of Hobbes situations owes much to Gauthier's article. Since I have changed some of the terminology and emphasis in my exposition of these ideas, I should be held responsible for any shortcomings in the discussion that follows.

his own advantage are not apt to lead an individual to conform to
B in what he takes to be a Hobbes situation. Moreover, the
structure of a Hobbes situation is such that unless he is confident
that there will be general conformity to B, he will see that he has
nothing to gain and possibly a great deal to lose from conforming
himself. It is important, therefore, in order to have enough conformity to secure the general benefit of the practice that most
individuals concerned are confident that enough other people
will conform to realize the general benefit.

Competitions, joint undertakings, and disarmament treaties
frequently have the characteristics of Hobbes situations. A
human community approximates a large Hobbes situation, or at
least, as Hobbes suggests, it so appears to many people.[5] For this
reason, many useful social arrangements are potentially unstable.
One function of certain forms of conscientiousness is to motivate
individuals to behave in generally beneficial ways in such situations. One reason why people are concerned about the characters
of other people is that so much depends upon enough people
being motivated in the desired ways.

Under the following conditions, there could be a stable, mutually beneficial practice, despite the fact that the individuals concerned have a strong concern for their own interests, the situation
is a Hobbes situation, and the practice is the relevant B.

(1) Most of the individuals in the situation are committed to
     conformity to B.

(2) They feel that except in quite special circumstances they
     have to conform to B whether they want to or not, even
     when this is disadvantageous to them.

---

5. In his reply to "the fool" who thinks it is sometimes advantageous to break
covenants (*Leviathan*, chap. 15), Hobbes argues that it is always imprudent to
break a valid covenant. If this is so, then the natural condition is not a Hobbes
situation, because condition (2) does not obtain. If, however, enough people
think that (2) obtains—if enough *think* that it is a Hobbes situation, the effect is
the same. Hobbes apparently thought that we are well supplied with fools. For
an interesting discussion of Hobbes's reply to "the fool," see D. Gauthier, *The
Logic of Leviathan* (Oxford: Clarendon Press, 1969), pp. 76–89.

(3) These individuals know of one another's commitment to *B*.

Certain forms of conscientiousness can perform the function of motivating people to observe generally beneficial forms of behavior in Hobbes situations. My thesis is that honesty, truthfulness, fairness, and being a person of one's word are forms of conscientiousness, and so motivating people is one of their most important functions.

To make stable the practice of conformity to *B*, we do not always rely only upon the conscientiousness of the participants to secure the desired degree of conformity. Thus, there are frequently procedures, formal and informal, to penalize nonconformity and reward conformity. There are laws and legal sanctions, efforts to exclude from Hobbes situations those who will not conform, etc. Notorious liars are not believed, and thus are thwarted in their attempts to profit by misrepresentation; cheaters are disqualified from competitions when they are detected, and we do not enter into agreements and cooperative ventures with those who break their word or take more than their share. These features tend to make such situations less than pure Hobbes situations, because an individual in the situation may not always be able to maximize his own advantage by nonconformity.

Some have thought that these procedures for encouraging conformity are by themselves sufficient to make it more advantageous for an individual to keep his word, to refrain from cheating, etc., when most others conform. Thus, on this view, our mutually beneficial moral and social practices are not properly regarded as Hobbes situations; the sanctions, formal and informal, against nonconformity have the result that condition (2) for a Hobbes situation is not fulfilled. One cannot reasonably expect to maximize one's advantage in such situations by not conforming when most others conform.[6]

---

6. See, for example, Philippa Foot, "Moral Beliefs," *Proceedings of the Aristotelian Society*, 59 (1958–1959), pp. 83–104.

Conscientiousness

Many of us believe that we are from time to time in situations in which we can profit from discreet cheating, lying, etc. I think, too, that such beliefs are substantially correct, and if so, the virtues that are forms of conscientiousness have an important function. Even if I am mistaken in believing that we are confronted with such situations, it is clear that many people subscribe to this belief.[7] Thus, considerations of an individual's own advantage could not by themselves be counted upon consistently to insure our conformity to certain generally beneficial forms of behavior. Hobbes's political solution to this difficulty is not very promising. On the other hand, a conscientious commitment to such forms of behavior as keeping one's word, taking no more than one's share, avoiding cheating, telling the truth under oath, etc., will provide the motivation to conform.

The notion of a Hobbes situation is properly regarded as an idealization more or less approximated in actual social situations. It is an idealization like ideal gases, frictionless planes, and point masses. It models a tendency for individual goals and community goals to clash with one another. A function of virtues that are forms of conscientiousness is to resolve this opposition in individuals in a way that is beneficial to individuals and communities.

How, in detail, the behavior characteristic of such particular virtues as honesty coincides with generally beneficial sorts of behavior in Hobbes situations will be considered in section 4 of this chapter. The subject of the next section is the thesis that

---

7. Proponents of the thesis that morality pays in this life—Plato, Hobbes, and Foot, for example—seem to hold this thesis because of their view of practical reason. All three suppose that in order to show how a course of action is reasonable for an individual, one must show that he can expect to profit from it, to get something that he wants at a reasonable cost. Thus each subscribes to some such conditional as: If it is reasonable for one to act justly, then by acting justly, one can expect to profit. Plato, Hobbes, and Foot affirm the antecedent of this conditional and infer the thesis that justice pays. In section 5 of this chapter, I reject this view of practical reason. Without such a priori argument, the thesis that morality always pays would not have many adherents. Most people would not find it a compelling induction from their own experience.

these forms of conscientiousness perform this useful function better than would certain other virtues.

3. *The Inseparability of Good and Ill*

Any sort of concern for the common good or for the general welfare is prima facie a candidate for performing the function attributed in the last section to some forms of conscientiousness. The deep-seated desire to ameliorate suffering and to promote the well-being of all sentient creatures, whether it takes the form of love or of a conscientious commitment to the principle "Maximize utility," might motivate individuals to conform to generally beneficial forms of behavior in Hobbes situations.

It was David Hume's idea, however, that some useful practices and institutions such as promising and property are governed by rules that in some cases prescribe actions contrary both to the interest of the agent and to the public interest. Thus in some situations, if Hume was right, one's benevolent inclinations might conflict with these rules. It was Hume's contention, nonetheless, that conscientious observance of such rules in a community would have better results on the whole than a general practice of following the promptings of benevolence.

A single act of justice is frequently contrary to *public interest*; and were it to stand alone, without being followed by other acts, may in itself be very prejudicial to society. . . . But however single acts of justice may be contrary either to public or to private interest, it is certain that the whole plan or scheme is highly conducive, or indeed absolutely requisite, both to the support of society and the well-being of every individual. It is impossible to separate the good from the ill. Property must be stable and must be fixed by general rules. Though in one instance the public be a sufferer, this momentary ill is amply compensated by the steady prosecution of the rule and by the peace and order which it establishes in society.[8]

A similar point is made by John Rawls about promising, with a clearer explanation than Hume's of why the good of such prac-

8. David Hume, *A Treatise of Human Nature*, L. A. Selby-Bigge, ed. (Oxford: Clarendon Press, 1888) p. 497. In the passage quoted, spelling and punctuation have been modernized.

tices is inseparable from the ill. "The point of the practice [of promising] is to abdicate one's title to act in accordance with utilitarian and prudential considerations in order that the future may be tied down and plans coordinated in advance. There are obvious utilitarian advantages in having a practice which denies to the promisor, as a defense, any general appeal to the utilitarian principle in accordance with which the practice itself may be justified."[9]

These views of Hume and Rawls suggest a second hypothesis about the functions of honesty, fairness, etc. These forms of conscientiousness motivate people to observe generally beneficial forms of behavior to which they would not consistently conform if they were motivated only by kindness, compassion, or even a conscientious adherence to the principle "Maximize utility." This hypothesis suggests an explanation for why there should be virtues that involve a direct concern with forms of behavior. If the hypothesis is correct, then the behavior of a truthful, honest, fair, trustworthy person is apt to be different from and preferable to the behavior of an act utilitarian.

Hume and Rawls are, I think, right on this point. Moreover, the same sort of point can be made about a wide variety of practices and institutions. There appears, however, to be a fatal objection to this idea. The objection is made from a utilitarian point of view, but Hume and Rawls appear to accept the premises of the objection in their defense of this idea.

The objection goes like this: Hume and Rawls admit the existence of a class of cases, C, in which the rules they advocate require that people do something other than maximize utility. Their rules, R, are so constructed that we are sometimes directed to do one thing even though utility would be maximized in the circumstances by doing something else. Their justification for these rules, however, is utilitarian; human needs and interests are better served by the general observance of R than they would be by the general observance of the rule "Maximize utility" (here-

9. John Rawls, "Two Concepts of Rules," *Philosophical Review*, 64 (1955), 16.

after, *MU*). The objection is that there seems to be an obvious way to revise the rules *R* to obtain rules whose general observance will result in even more utility. *R'* is a set of rules identical to *R* except that the rules *R'* direct that in cases belonging to class *C*, utility is to be maximized. Since this is the *only* difference between *R* and *R'*, the observance of *R'* should result in *more* utility than the observance of *R*. *R* and *R'* prescribe the *same* courses of action in all cases except for those in class *C*. In these cases, *R'* prescribes the maximally optimific course, while *R* prescribes a different course—a course that in each case results in less utility. Thus, the general observance of *R'* will result in more utility than the general observance of *R*. This objection is meant to present a rule utilitarian such as Hume or the Rawls of "Two Concepts of Moral Rules" with a dilemma: he must either adopt a set of rules which, in effect, prescribe the same actions as *MU*, or he must find reasons other than strictly utilitarian ones for preferring *R* to *R'*. The moral seems to be that if one wants to be a utilitarian, one might as well be an act utilitarian. This objection makes it appear that a person motivated by benevolence to maximize utility in every case would be apt to do the same things as a person who conscientiously observes certain rules the general observance of which results in more utility than other rules.[10]

This objection, however, depends upon the assumption that revisions of the rules of certain practices would affect only the outcomes in individual cases to which the rules apply. The conclusion that more utility will result from the general observance of *R'* is based upon the assumption that the same or nearly the same number of acts would take place under *R'* as take place under *R*. The dubious nature of this assumption is clear in the case of promising. The rules that govern our present practice of promising, as Rawls maintains, require the promisor to abdicate his title to act in accordance with utilitarian considerations, except when the consequences of keeping his promise are extremely severe. In some cases, therefore, these rules require the promisor

10. This objection is developed by David Lyons in *Forms and Limits of Utilitarianism* (Oxford: Clarendon Press, 1965), 185–186.

to keep his promise even though the results would be somewhat better on the whole if he did not keep his promise. These are the cases C. We can imagine a different practice of promising in which the promisor is directed in such cases to break his promise and do whatever on the whole has the best results. Would the revised practice result in more good than the present one? If people were to use the revised practice as frequently as they use the present one, and if they used it in the same situations, and if all else remained the same, then simple arithmetic shows that more good would be realized from the revised practice. Can we assume, though, that people would use the revised practice as frequently as they use the existing practice? Would not the revised practice be a *less useful* tool for our purposes than the existing practice? Rawls observes that "the point of the practice is to abdicate one's title to act in accordance with utilitarian and prudential considerations in order that the future may be tied down and plans coordinated in advance." The existing practice of promising does this better than would the revised practice. Often people make mutual promises—enter into agreements—in situations in which it is not clear what all the results will be of keeping the promises. If each can see from the outset that he has something to lose if the others do not keep their promises, then the willingness of each to enter into the agreement and risk the loss will depend upon his confidence that the others' promises tie them down. Where this confidence is lacking, then the beneficial results of cooperation requiring mutual promising is apt to be lost, all because the promises are not made.

Hume's rule utilitarian account of property can be defended against the revisionist's objection in the same way. Existing rules of property require us in some cases to do something other than maximize utility. No doubt these rules are undergoing revision all the time, and it cannot be denied that certain revisions are desirable. The act utilitarian-revisionist, however, advocates revising these rules so that in every case we are required to maximize utility. He points out that if rules revised in this way had guided people in the cases C, then more utility would have resulted than did result from our existing practices with respect to

property. We cannot assume, however, that if this revised institu-
tion of property had been in effect, all would have gone as before
with the cases other than those in class C. It is plausible to
suppose that under the rules the revisionist proposes, property
would be less useful and desirable. If so, people would be less
willing to produce and maintain things. Things would be worse
rather than better.

Utilitarians have a tendency to think of alternative practices as
coin-operated machines that pay off in units of good. One simply
chooses the machine with the biggest payoff. Practices and institutions, however, have specific uses and purposes in a complicated form of social life. It is better to think of them as tools and
consider how well suited they are to fulfill certain purposes.
Utilitarianism leads one to ask 'How much good would result
from such and such a practice?' which is not a very good question. One should ask instead, at least to begin with, 'How satisfactory would the practice be for such and such purposes?'

This revisionist objection assumes that the rules revised in the
way proposed would define an alternative practice in some in-
telligible way. In my defense of Hume and Rawls against this
objection, I have conceded this assumption. There is good reason, however, to be skeptical about this assumption. Suppose that
the local chess club decreed that within its precincts, wherever
utility could be maximized by departing from the rules of chess,
players are required to do so. My defense is analogous to the
observation in this case that if the chess club did this, it would
lose membership, because fewer people would want to play chess
under the revised rules. We might wonder, however, what on
earth the remaining members would do under this odd rule.

Part of the difficulty here lies in the unclarity of what one is
supposed to be doing in maximizing utility. If we are trying to
satisfy as many of the desires of as many people as possible, we
must keep in mind that people have many of the desires they do
because of the form of life they lead. Of course, their lives are
structured by the conventions, the rules and practices, of their
communities. If we think in terms of maximizing the satisfaction
of desires we presently have, then the strategy of the wholesale

abandonment of these conventions or even a very sweeping revision of them is not very promising. If, however, we think of maximizing *other* desires that are not tied to the way of life we presently lead, we do not yet know what these desires are, let alone what to do to satisfy them.

A conscientious commitment to certain forms of behavior—those prescribed by the rules that govern our practices with respect to promising and property, for example—will be desirable if general conformity to those forms is desirable. Honesty, fairness, being a person of one's word, and truthfulness are not functionally equivalent in a community to such traits as kindness and benevolence, even when these lead a person to be governed in all things by the rule "Maximize utility." Assuming that Hume and Rawls are correct about promising and property, and that a similar point can be made about other moral and social institutions and practices—for example laws, giving help to those in distress, various kinds of competitions—then we are better off if people generally behave in ways fully characteristic of the appropriate forms of conscientiousness than if people in these situations simply try to be as benevolent as possible.

If an individual who is committed to the principle "Maximize utility" could be convinced by such arguments as these, his response might be that he should publicly advocate conformity to such useful practices, while privately adhering to MU. This strategy would lead him to violate the rules of those practices when MU so directed and when he could do so without setting a bad example. This was Henry Sidgwick's view. "On Utilitarian principles, it may be right to do and privately recommend, under certain circumstances, what it would not be right to advocate openly; . . . it may be conceivably right to do, if it can be done with comparative secrecy, what it would be wrong to do in the face of the world. . . . A Utilitarian may reasonably desire, on Utilitarian principles, that some of his conclusions should be rejected by mankind generally."[11]

This view is analogous to the response to the argument in

11. Henry Sidgwick, *The Methods of Ethics*, pp. 489–490.

section 2 of this chapter that someone who wishes to maximize his own advantage should in Hobbes situations advocate and encourage others to conform to generally beneficial forms of behavior while secretly not conforming when it is advantageous for him. A quick answer to both Sidgwick and the egoist on these points is that their secret nonconformity will, more often than not, be wrong. They will wrong individuals who trust them to act in good faith, individuals who reasonably expect their conformity. I will try to show the reasonableness of such an answer in section 5 below.

Utilitarians such as Sidgwick often suppose that in view of the strong feelings that people have about violations of trust, etc., and in view of the pain that individuals are apt to feel when they are wronged, an enlightened utilitarian will be very cautious about not conforming to conventional morality. Thus a utilitarian can often manage to be conventionally good without being untrue to his principle. To whatever degree it exists, however, the congruence between utilitarian practice in accordance with *MU* and the practice of individuals who are conscientious about promising, property, etc., depends upon the fact that many people *are* conscientious about these matters and *do* feel strongly about violations. These attitudes are not altogether reasonable from a utilitarian point of view. Yet the plausibility that utilitarianism derives from its congruence with existing moral practices is parasitic upon the existence of a community with attitudes and values that are not utilitarian. Without these attitudes and values, many useful moral and social institutions we have, such as promising and property, would not exist in their present useful form. Utilitarians such as Sidgwick find themselves in the odd position of being grateful for the existence of practices and attitudes that, on their view, are not altogether reasonable. The difficulty here, I think, lies in the utilitarian conception of reasonableness in practical affairs. If the attitudes characteristic of those who possess virtues that are forms of conscientiousness can be shown to be reasonable, then *MU* is not the touchstone of reason. A utilitarian may get by in life following *MU*, but he will not properly understand and appreciate the attitudes and values of his fellows. Such a failure of understanding could lead him to err in important practical matters. If utilitarianism is mistaken in this way, then it is important to abandon *MU* as a practical principle.

4. *Honesty*

It has been asserted that honesty, truthfulness, being a person of one's word, and fairness are forms of conscientiousness that fulfill certain socially useful functions, but the discussion so far has been general and schematic. This section takes up a particular virtue, honesty, conceived as a form of conscientiousness.

Being honest has to do with being trustworthy, but not every case of keeping a trust is a case of being honest. If, for example, I am told something in confidence, and I keep the confidence, I am being trustworthy, but not necessarily honest. Again, if someone makes an agreement, intending to keep it, but then changes his mind, it would not be dishonest openly to refuse to keep the agreement. It would be a breach of faith, but not an instance of dishonesty. To make an agreement, however, which from the very outset one has no intention of keeping, leading the other party to believe that one intends to keep the agreement, is a dishonest performance. Characteristically, cases of dishonesty involve an attempt to deceive. The highwayman is not, as a rule, being dishonest as he plies his trade, whereas the confidence man, the embezzler, and often the sneak-thief are being dishonest. The child who stealthily takes money from his mother's purse is liable to get a lecture on honesty if he is caught, whereas the burglar who steals from an empty house after breaking in is not being dishonest. The child is in a position of trust with respect to those from whom he steals, and he pretends to deserve that trust, so that he can take advantage of those who trust him by violating that trust. The burglar is not in any such position; in committing his crime he does not pretend to be anything he is not. He is an honest criminal, unlike the shoplifter who poses as a customer.

Obviously, not just any attempt to deceive is dishonest. *Trompe l'oeil* painters are not necessarily dishonest, nor are people who tell white lies. It is wrongful deceptions that are dishonest, but not all wrongful deceptions are dishonest. A malicious prankster deceives motorists by placing a detour sign in such a way that they are led onto the wrong road. "Dishonest" does not seem the right word for what he has done. The prankster has not taken advantage of others' trust of him; he is not abusing others' trust *in him* in the way characteristic of dishonesty. The dishonest person uses others' trust of him to get into a position where he can violate that trust in a way that advances his own purposes. One such situation would be a Hobbes situation. In acting dishonestly, one might be intending to decieve some person or persons into thinking that one is conforming to *B* in a Hobbes situation, when in fact one is not conforming, and one is thereby attempting to secure one's own maximum advantage by enjoying the benefits of the general conformity to *B* without suffering the inconveniences of adhering to *B* oneself.

It is not surprising that there is a special word, "dishonest," for those who try, by deceit, to advance their own aims in such situations. Frequently, the only way in a Hobbes situation both to enjoy the benefits of general conformity and to avoid the burdens of conformity oneself is to deceive others into thinking one is conforming. In fact, we do not trust to people's rectitude alone to insure their conformity. We punish those whose nonconformity is detected. We try to exclude from Hobbes situations those who we suspect will not conform. We try not to enter into agreements of mutual trust with those who are apt to take advantage of us by not performing their part. We shun joint enterprises with people who try to get a share of the fruits of the endeavor without shouldering their share of the burden. Thus someone who wishes to maximize his own advantage in a Hobbes situation often must at least seem to conform to *B* in order to be able to succeed. Where this pretense of conformity is used as a means of securing the trust of others as a part of a plan to advance one's own purposes by violating that trust, one is acting in a way fully characteristic of dishonesty. Such pretense typically is found in cheating in competitions, embezzlements, bearing false witness, and various kinds of frauds and swindles. The purposes a dishonest person seeks to advance are often selfish ones, but they might be benevolent, even altruistic.

An honest person is one who is committed to the avoidance of the sort of deceitful violations of trust commonly exemplified by cheating, etc. He feels that he must avoid such behavior because it is wrong, and the wrongness of such an action, for him, is independent of the results of the action. Being honest is not by itself enough to make a person trustworthy in agreements, joint enterprises, and other Hobbes situations. An honest person may renege on an agreement made in good faith when he later changes his mind. Insofar as he is honest, he will eschew deceit in benefiting from a violation of trust, but he may still openly break his agreement. It is a person of his word who is committed to keeping his agreements. One who is both honest and a person of his word still may live by violence and robbery. One might characterize as unfair someone who takes things by force from those to whom the things rightfully belong. The term "trustworthy" can be used to refer to the general commitment to be worthy of the trust of one's fellow human beings, and this form of conscientiousness is the genus of which fairness, honesty, truthfulness, and being a person of one's word are all more specific forms. The latter virtues, however, are not mutually exclusive species of trustworthiness. These virtues tend to overlap, and instances of meritorious truthfulness tend also to be instances of acting honestly, etc. It is possible, with a little ingenuity, to argue plausibly that any one of these specific virtues can be shown to be a special case of one of the others. For example, one might argue that cheating and taking more than one's share involve breaking an implicit agreement to adhere to certain forms of behavior. Alternatively, one might argue that these forms of behavior are *unfair* because one is attempting to enjoy the benefits of others' conformity to beneficial practices without shouldering one's own share of the burden. These concepts are flexible, and they are clearly very closely related.

The virtues that cluster around trustworthiness in this way are not the only forms of conscientiousness plausibly regarded as virtues. Anything that can be construed as a moral obligation is something one can be conscientious about—for example: rendering aid to people in distress when one can do so easily, avoiding causing pain and injury to others, and avoiding arousing expectations one does not intend to satisfy. Kindness and compassion are virtues that might lead one to do these things too. As Kant pointed out, however, it is entirely possible for someone who is for some reason *not* moved by sympathy for someone's plight to render aid because he thinks it would be wrong not to do so. Whether it is preferable to be sympathetic or conscientious about such matters will be discussed later. Such things as rendering aid and avoiding causing injury, however, can be seen as forms of behavior that are beneficial when their observance is general in a community but whose observance does involve some sacrifice and burden. If enough people are sufficiently conscientious about such things, then everyone is apt to benefit.

When I speak of the "benefits" of general adherence to such forms of behavior as avoiding cheating, keeping one's agreements, doing one's share, etc., I do not mean merely that such practices make life smoother and more pleasant than it would be otherwise. Such general practices are absolutely necessary in order to have communities, and thus they are necessary for the sort of life we regard as characteristically human.

5. *Conscientiousness and Reason*

In reply to the question 'Why should one do what is normally called one's duty?' Prichard answered, in effect, that it is just obviously so. One has no grounds, according to Prichard, nor does one need grounds. That one should do these things is self-evident.

Certain facts seem to support Prichard in this regard. When someone maintains that he should not cheat because cheating is wrong, it is not normal practice to call upon him to produce grounds for his belief. Such a person may be at a loss if he is asked to produce grounds, but this inability is unlikely to lead him to change his mind. It is as if he knows he needs no grounds. After all, it is common knowledge that such things are wrong.

Prichard contended that an honest person *cannot* produce satisfactory grounds for his belief that he should not cheat. All possible attempts, Prichard argued, will fail. The theory of the self-evidence of certain obligations was meant to account for the fact that the honest person lacks nothing necessary to make his belief well founded, even though he has no grounds.

It does seem possible, however, for the honest person to produce perfectly good reasons for his belief that cheating is wrong. He might say, for example, that when people play a game or compete with one another, they agree, often tacitly, to abide by certain rules. When someone cheats, he intentionally breaks the rules and thereby breaks his word. Alternatively, it could be argued that general observance of the rules is necessary in order to have a game or competition. One who does not follow the rules shirks his fair share of the burden that should fall equally on all players. Thus it is unfair to cheat. Either of these explanations, suitably elaborated, is a perfectly reasonable explanation of why cheating is wrong.

These explanations, however, assimilate the duty to avoid cheating to other kinds of duties, and Prichard's question was, 'Why should one do what is normally called one's duty?' The generality of Prichard's question places *all* duties among the phenomena to be explained. Neither these explanations, then, nor the ones Prichard examined and rejected are satisfactory for his purposes.

If one asks for an explanation or justification of something in a certain area, and if one frames the question in such a way that everything that can be cited in that area for purposes of explanation or justification falls under the scope of the question, then the task set by the question is impossible. Justifications have to come to an end, as Wittgenstein said, and it is not surprising that we can formulate requests for justifications that are so general that there is nothing left outside the boundary of the justificandum to serve as a justification. It is tempting to say that the answer a

conscientious person should give to Prichard's question is simply
that this is the kind of life we lead—period. He neither has nor
needs a justification, nor is anything gained by appealing to
"self-evidence." Wittgenstein said, "What people accept as a
justification—is shown by how they think and live," and "What
has to be accepted, the given is—so one could say—*forms of
life.*"[12]

The view I have just sketched is like Prichard's in one respect.
Both say, in effect, that we just have to accept the fact that we
should do these things we call "our duty." On Prichard's view,
however, we are justified in accepting this fact because it is self-
evident that we should do these things. A major difficulty with
this view is that we are given no account of self-evidence that will
enable us confidently to distinguish genuine from spurious self-
evidence. On the second view, we are not justified in thinking
that we should do these things, but there is no need for any
justification. The difficulty with this view is that it threatens to
obliterate the distinction between a reasoned moral view and the
pronouncements of a moral dogmatist. This sort of appeal to ways
of life that we must accept without justification makes justification itself seem hollow.

In the light of the discussions in the preceding sections, it does
seem possible to understand the functions of virtues that are
forms of conscientiousness and to understand why these traits are
prized. It is astounding, then, that there should be such difficulty
about *justifying* certain forms of conscientiousness—exhibiting
the reasonableness of a conscientious person's belief that he is
obliged to do certain things. If Hobbes situations are common in
our lives, and if certain forms of conscientiousness are best suited
to motivate people to conform to the mutually beneficial forms of
behavior in these situations, then the desirability of as many
people as possible possessing those traits is manifest. Prichard
would argue, though, that such considerations might make
someone *want* to be conscientious, but it would not show

12. Ludwig Wittgenstein, *Philosophical Investigations*, Part I, §325, p. 106e,
and Part II, § xi, p. 226e. I do not mean to suggest that Wittgenstein would
necessarily have approved of using these remarks in this way.

that he is *obliged* to do anything. These considerations show the desirability of widespread possession of certain character traits, but they do not show that any particular person has to conform to a certain form of behavior. In a true Hobbes situation, it is most advantageous for an individual not to conform, no matter what other people do. Finally, a conscientious person's belief that he has to conform to a certain mode of behavior does not rest upon the belief that something good invariably results from each instance of that behavior, according to Prichard. These points fit with the results of the last two sections: actions fully characteristic of honesty, etc., may be contrary to the interests of those affected by the actions. The conscientious person cannot point to the results of his action to explain why he thinks he is obliged so to act. All he can say, Prichard concluded, is, "I am required to do this action," and if his belief is well founded, it can only be because that he is required to do the action *is* self-evident.

In this argument, Prichard overlooked another way in which the conscientious person's belief might be shown to be reasonable. Prichard overlooked it because he shared with Hume and many others certain assumptions about the role of reasoning in practical matters. There is a tendency to take as *the* paradigm of practical reasoning an individual's trying to figure out how to get what he wants. Good practical reasoning is conceived exclusively as discerning the most effective and efficient means to the desired end. The rationality of pursuing the end may come into question by asking how its pursuit may affect one's chances of getting other things that one wants, but the pattern here is fundamentally the same. The reasonableness of one's pursuit of a particular end is assessed in terms of its conduciveness to other ends one desires. If one desires something for its own sake, however, then this desire itself is neither reasonable nor unreasonable. If one pursues this end desired for its own sake, such a course might be unreasonable if it obviously interfered with the pursuit of *other* ends that rank higher on one's personal preference scale. If, however, one is committed to a certain form of behavior in the way in which a conscientious person is, and conforming to this way of behaving is not desired for the sake of something else, then one cannot show the reasonableness of *this* commitment by showing that it conduces to some other end that one has. At this point, it seems that the most one can say is, "I have a strong desire to act in this way for its own sake, but I have no further reason." This explanation, however, will not account for one's belief that one has to or is obliged to act in this way. Such a belief should be sustained by reasons, and the fact that one wants to act in a certain way does not support the claim that one is obliged to do it. Prichard's response at this point is to proclaim the self-evidence of the belief that one is obliged to do such things.

This sort of account of how a person properly decides what to do is unsatisfactory in certain respects.[13] The crucial mistake in Prichard's argument, however, is his acceptance of a view of practical reasoning based upon the assumption that questions of reasonableness in practical matters arise *only* in connection with an individual's deciding what he wants and how to get it. There are other ways, however, in which reasonableness can become a consideration in action, and one of these ways provides the basis for a justification of conscientiousness that avoids Prichard's predicament.

Prichard's (and Hume's) paradigm of practical reasoning takes place with a solitary deliberator. Consider instead a case involving two people in which one asks, requires, or demands something of the other. Such requests, demands, or requirements can be assessed as reasonable or unreasonable. If person A *reasonably* asks something of person B, then the reasonableness of the request gives B *a reason for complying*, quite apart from B's plans and goals. This reason for complying can be overridden by other considerations, but it is itself a consideration to be taken into account. In the absence of overriding considerations, if A reasonably asks something of B, then there are grounds for holding that B should comply. He should comply because something is reasonably asked of him.

13. For a discussion, see my "Practical Inquiry," *Philosophical Review*, 78 (1969), 435–450.

Conscientiousness

It is very common for a group of people to *require* things of one another. When a club has rules—written or unwritten—to govern the association of the members with one another and the conduct of their business, the rules can be taken as statements of what the members require of one another. These requirements too can be assessed as reasonable or unreasonable in the light of the purposes of the association, the internal circumstances of the club, and the larger social setting in which the club exists. Where those requirements are reasonable, there are grounds for the claim that members of the club have to observe them.

The discussions of the useful functions of virtues that are forms of conscientiousness in sections 2 through 4 above can be taken as accounts of why it is reasonable for us, collectively, as a community, to require of one another adherence to certain generally beneficial forms of behavior. A community does require things of its members—otherwise it would not be a community. If all is well, then often these requirements will be reasonable.

The form of the argument for the reasonableness of such requirements as promise keeping, truth telling, doing one's share, etc., is *not:* You should conform to certain modes of behavior because so doing will have certain results which you want. This argument will fail because a particular individual's adherence to this way of behaving is neither necessary nor sufficient for his deriving the benefits of these practices. Moreover, adherence to the practice sometimes will require him to sacrifice his interests. In all likelihood, he can enjoy the benefits of the general conformity without always conforming himself. The argument, much compressed, for the reasonableness of requiring of one another conformity to these forms of behavior is this: General conformity in our community to certain modes of behavior is enormously beneficial, and these benefits are very widely distributed. The sacrifices individuals must make to conform to these modes of behavior are generally small in comparison with these benefits. It is therefore reasonable for us to require of one another conformity to these modes of behavior. Each of us is thus reasonably required to refrain from cheating, to keep agreements, etc. One should do these things, therefore, not because of the results of one's so doing, but because they are reasonably required of one by the community of which one is a member.

Such arguments as these are defeasible. If, for example, general conformity to certain beneficial modes of behavior resulted in an unfair distribution of benefits and burdens, then this circumstance might defeat the argument in the preceding paragraph. Of course, it might not, too. Some injustices may be tolerable, especially if they are slight and few and the benefits of the practice enormous. Reasonable people differ about the desirability of "strict liability" for certain legal offenses, even though all agree that injustices result from such laws.

That it is reasonable for us to require of one another conformity to a certain mode of behavior does not entail that it would be desirable to coerce anyone into conforming to that mode of behavior. These are separate matters.

In this way, the considerations in sections 2 through 4 can be advanced by an honest person in support of his belief that he has to avoid cheating and other actions involving wrongful deceptions. He can, in this way, defend the reasonableness of his view and turn aside the criticism that his conscientiousness about the matter is fundamentally a nonrational commitment.

The accounts of conscientiousness offered by such intuitionists as Prichard and W. David Ross invite the following sort of objection. "The doctrine of the purely conscientious act is irrational. This doctrine holds, first, that the highest moral motive is the desire to do what is right and just simply because it is right and just, *no other description being appropriate....* But on this interpretation the sense of right lacks any apparent reason; it resembles a preference for tea rather than coffee. Although such a preference might exist, to make it regulative of the basic structure of society is utterly capricious."[14]

Prichard might reply that the self-evidence of the obligatoriness

---

14. John Rawls, A *Theory of Justice,* pp. 477–478. The emphasis is mine.

of "right action" makes any further reason for such actions super-fluous, but the doctrine of self-evidence is too weak to bear such weight. A conscientious person can say more than just that cheat-ing is wrong and that it must be avoided. He can say that we are reasonably required not to cheat, and then proceed to argue for the reasonableness of the requirement. On this amended view of a conscientious act, it does not lack a reason, and the fitness of virtues that are forms of conscientiousness for the function of social regulation are to be found in the rationale. An act fully characteristic of honesty, a conscientious act, *need not* be done simply because the act is right, *no other description being appropriate.* The fact that the agent refrains from cheating because it is reasonably required of him makes the description, "doing what is reasonably required of me," part of his reason for so acting.

It might be objected that such a person is no longer *intrinsically* motivated in avoiding cheating, etc. The fact that the action is reasonably required of him motivates him, on this account, and not the character of the action itself. This last point, of course, is correct. It is important to keep in mind, however, that such a person is motivated by the fact that the action is reasonably required of him and *not* by the fact that his so acting will have certain results.

Is such a person *intrinsically* motivated? Perhaps not in the sense that some intuitionists have had in mind when they spoke of a sense of duty or right. One is not motivated to avoid cheat-ing by some simple, unanalyzable characteristic of such actions. This, however, is a view adopted only out of desperation. Such virtues as honesty, truthfulness, fairness, and being a person of one's word are "artificial virtues" in Hume's terminology. The actions fully characteristic of these virtues require for their per-formance a certain setting that involves complex conventions. The notion that our attitudes toward such actions can be ex-plained without reference to a social context is implausible. If one understands "intrinsic" as the contrary of "instrumental," however, then matters are different. In this sense, an honest person who avoids cheating because this kind of behavior is reasonably required of him and not just because his so acting has results that he desires is intrinsically motivated. This view preserves the most important and plausible aspects of a deontological account of these virtues, while at the same time providing access to certain of the relevant considerations advanced by teleological accounts in order to show the reasonableness of the attitudes connected with these virtues. The account reconciles plausible aspects of both kinds of theories while avoiding certain of their difficulties.

This is not to say that all people who are honest, fair, truthful, etc., are so because they see the reasonableness of these requirements, though I do suspect that such requirements would not be taken seriously if there were not good reasons for them. Someone may be perfectly honest who believes that avoiding cheating is required of him by God or by a priori moral law. Intuitionists and noncognitivists may possess these virtues. I am not claiming, either, that individuals who are dishonest, grasping, mendacious, etc., are always so because of ignorance of these considerations or unreasonable failure to draw a conclusion that follows from premises they accept. I take this, rather, to show that the conscientious person's belief that he has to observe the appropriate forms of behavior can be supported by cogent reasons and in that sense shown to be reasonable. There are grounds, whether he realizes it or not, that he can adduce in support of his belief that he ought to act in these ways, grounds that will support these beliefs without turning them into hypothetical imperatives. These grounds are cogent, and thus they should convince anyone that he ought to avoid cheating, to keep his promises, etc. This is not to say that these grounds will convince him. Still, someone who does not see the grounds for the honest person's beliefs about what he has to do is missing something, and someone who denies that these are grounds is mistaken. The possible sources of such a mistake are many.

6. *Conscientiousness and Judgment*

The attitudes characteristic of honesty, fairness, truthfulness, and being a person of one's word can be shown to be reasonable, even though the individuals who are conscientious in these ways may be unable to articulate the considerations that make these attitudes reasonable. Nonetheless, the fact that an action of a sort an individual is conscientious about is one of his options on a given occasion is itself an important consideration for him, and it is *a consideration* independent of the anticipated consequences of so acting for his own plans or the interests of others. Of course, his own purposes and the interests of others may be considerations too, and these may be weightier considerations than the behavior indicated by conscientiousness. That a person has the virtues that are forms of conscientiousness does not spare him from making decisions, sometimes difficult, where there are conflicting considerations. The possession of such virtues obviously is not enough by itself. In the absence of good judgment, these traits may constitute the character of a person who would be, at best, an irritating prig and, at worst, a dangerous fanatic.

It may appear that we should now undertake the task of listing the important considerations in life and ranking them in order of importance, indicating the place in that ranking of actions fully characteristic of honesty, etc. This, however, cannot be done. The question "Generally, how important is the fact that one made a promise?" deserves the same answer as the question "Generally, how much does a stone weigh?" Notice, however, that the unmanageability of the former question no more precludes determining the importance of a *particular* promise than the unmanageability of the latter question precludes the determination of the weight of a particular stone. It is interesting to note, too, that in practice, intuition is not particularly useful or reliable in either sort of determination.

The analogy between weighing considerations and weighing stones may suggest that for the former kind of determination, as for the latter, we can describe a general procedure that can be used in particular cases to produce the desired determinations. In fact, though, there is such an enormous diversity of considerations and situations in human affairs, that the idea of a general procedure for making all such determinations is most unpromising. Measuring, for example, is a common form of determination, but there is an absolutely bewildering variety of methods and techniques of measuring. Very different kinds of quantities are measured: distances, volumes, pressures, specific gravities, acidities, angles, times, economic values, and aptitudes, to mention only a few. Even the same kind of quantity is apt to be measured in very different ways in different circumstances. Consider the different ways in which the mass of a star, a boulder, and an electron are measured. Measuring, extensive and heterogeneous as it is, is a very small area of endeavor in comparison with the range and variety of problems and situations encountered in human life generally. Measurement is simply one special kind of determination relevant to practical problems. Determination of the importance of considerations ranges over all practical problems in all areas of human life. Moral considerations may be relevant in any area of life. The notion that we can describe *a* decision procedure for determining all kinds of measurements is implausible because of the indefinitely many methods of measuring in actual life. Yet the idea of a decision procedure for *any* and *all* practical problems—an algorithm for dealing with all considerations relevant to the decisions that we must make—is incomparably more implausible.

A. E. Murphy discussed the idea that we can enunciate moral laws that are "unconditionally applicable in all situations."

This might be done by including in the law itself all allowable exceptions. Promises are always to be kept unless—with a list of all allowable exceptions.... But for moral purposes [this] is both theoretically and practically futile. The complexity of specific situations is such that no list of exceptions, drawn up in advance, will actually cover all morally questionable cases.... But the more fundamental question is that of how the exceptions, the 'unlesses,' are got into the rule in the first place. Here somebody must make a judgment on what the exceptions ought to be.... *How* is he to judge?[15]

The difficulty in constructing decision procedures for all practical problems is not due only to the variety and complexity of

15. Arthur E. Murphy, *The Theory of Practical Reason* (La Salle, Ill.: Open Court, 1964), pp. 117–118.

these problems. Things change, and new situations for which we are not prepared are continually encountered. New situations tend to present the most interesting, challenging, and difficult problems. In criticizing theories of knowledge that attempt to offer a universal pattern for all acceptable rational inquiry, Frederick L. Will makes the point that such accounts cannot countenance as rational the sorts of radical revision and correction of knowledge that are among the greatest achievements of human intellectual history. Of the problems that lead to such revisions, he says,

These are not questions that can be answered, once for all, in some broad prolegomenon to epistemology and metaphysics, by the determination of one correct-for-all-time set of procedures, by the devising of a similarly immune-from-change-and-revision "ideal" language, a similarly philosophically congealed "system of concepts." As life changes, as the forms of cognitive life extending from common sense to the most advanced intellectual disciplines change, our procedures, language, forms of discrimination and thought undergo revision and change.[16]

These points apply to practical problems in all areas of life. We have continually to devise new ways of dealing with problems. The notion that we can find an algorithm for solving all practical problems involves the additional implausible assumption that we can anticipate ahead of time all future novel, unprecedented problems and, in effect, solve them in advance.

7. The Unity of Virtue

There has been a wide divergence of opinion among philosophers about the value and importance of virtues that are forms of conscientiousness. Kant maintained that only acts done "from duty" have "moral worth." Acts motivated by sympathy and kindness, he allowed, might be praiseworthy, but such acts do not reflect *moral* credit upon the agent. Only if the agent does his duty for its own sake, according to Kant, is he deserving of moral praise. Such a person finds in himself "a worth far higher

16. *Induction and Justification* (Ithaca, N.Y.: Cornell University Press, 1974), p. 240.

than any good natured temperament can have." "It is precisely in this that the worth of character begins to show—a moral worth and beyond all comparison the highest—namely, that he does good, not from inclination, but from duty."[17]

It was Kant's view, in other words, that only acts fully characteristic of a virtue that is a form of conscientiousness will reflect *moral* credit upon an agent. This implies that *moral* character is made up exclusively of forms of conscientiousness. Since Kant maintained that there is but one "supreme principle of morality," the upshot is that a morally good person is one who conscientiously adheres to this principle.

Prichard, like Kant, saw *moral* character as a matter of conscientiousness about obligation. "We must sharply distinguish morality and virtue as independent, though related, species of goodness. . . . An act, to be virtuous, must, as Aristotle saw, be done willingly or with pleasure; as such it is just not done from a sense of obligation but from some desire which is intrinsically good. . . . The goodness of such an act is different from the goodness of an act to which we apply the term moral in the strict and narrow sense, viz. an act done from a sense of obligation."[18]

Prichard and Kant seem pretty much in agreement about what sort of thing is properly called moral, but Prichard did not share Kant's view that conscientiousness about duty is a moral worth of character "beyond all comparison the highest." Moral philosophy seemed to Prichard remote from actual life. In discussing this he remarked: "Is not this largely because, while Moral Philosophy has, quite rightly, concentrated its attention on the fact of obligation, in the case of many of those whom we admire most and whose lives are of the greatest interest, the sense of obligation, though it may be an important, is not a dominating factor in their lives?"[19]

17. H. J. Paton, trans., *The Moral Law: Kant's Groundwork of the Metaphysic of Morals* (London: Hutchinson, 1948), p. 66.
18. *Moral Obligation*, pp. 11–12.
19. *Moral Obligation*, p. 12n. This idea is discussed in W. K. Frankena, "Prichard and the Ethics of Virtue," *The Monist*, 54 (1970), 1–17.

Conscientiousness

At the other extreme from Kant, P. H. Nowell-Smith expressed the opinion that a sense of duty is neither the only nor the highest moral virtue. "The sense of duty is a useful device for helping men to do what a really good man would do without a sense of duty; and, since none of us belongs to the class of "really good men" in this sense, it is a motive that should be fostered in all of us. But it plays little part in the lives of the best men and could play none at all in the lives of saints. They act on good moral principles, but not from the sense of duty; for they do what they do for its own sake and not for the sake of duty."[20]

A well-worn analogy seems to me to capture the structure and plausibility of Nowell-Smith's view. Consider the case of a parent who is lacking in affection for his child but who takes seriously his obligations as a parent. His sense of duty, we might say, leads him to do what a really good parent would do out of affection for his child. Still, he is not a really good parent; he is lacking in something that he, as a parent, should have. Nowell-Smith makes a similar point about a "really good man."

What desire or desires could a good person have, however, that would lead him to do what a person with a sense of duty would do? What could play the role in the case of the "really good man" that is played in the case of the good parent by affection for his children? Nowell-Smith does not say. Sympathy, fellow-feeling, kindness, and compassion might be suggested for this role. It does seem that a person who helps others from a sense of duty but who never feels any (other) inclination to help them is lacking in something that a really good person would have. If a truly good person is, among other things, a kind, compassionate, and generous person, then someone who lacks these virtues is not truly good. It does not follow from this, however, that conscientiousness is everywhere a second-best substitute for true goodness. In certain cases in which others need our help, both duty and compassion bid us render aid. We have seen, however, that benevo-

20. *Ethics*, p. 259.

lence will not in all cases result in the same behavior as honesty, fairness, truthfulness, and being a person of one's word.

In response to Nowell-Smith on this point, Kurt Baier says, "It would seem to be quite impossible for a person to be so endowed with natural inclinations (however complicated we envisage his 'programming' to be) that he would be inclined to do *anyway* all those things (under their morally neutral descriptions, e.g. to deliver milk, bread, wood, etc.) which he comes to be required to do only as a result of having entered into such specific relationships with others. And if he were so endowed, such commitments would be completely superflous. Moreover, he would be prevented from committing himself in certain ways in which he is not in fact so prevented: he would be prevented from committing himself or from becoming committed in all those ways which would go counter to his natural inclinations whatever they may be."[21]

It is not self-contradictory to say that a certain person has all of the right desires so that he always naturally wants, more than he wants anything else, to do what an honest, fair, etc., person would do, so that having the virtues that are forms of conscientiousness is unnecessary for him. The supposition that there is such a person, however, is of the same order of improbability as the supposition that there is a person who just naturally has all of the right thoughts in the right order, so that learning, inquiry, the rules of right reasoning and methodology, and intellectual discipline are unnecessary for him. Moral institutions and practices, like intellectual disciplines and methods of inquiry, give highly complex structures to individuals' thoughts and desires, which serve human purposes in a great many ways. The idea that an individual just might naturally find his thoughts and desires falling into these complex patterns without the operation of the forces designed to produce them is fantastic.

The virtues that are forms of conscientiousness, then, are not second-best substitutes for "true virtue" any more than a disci-

---

21. "Moral Value and Moral Worth," *The Monist,* 54 (1970), 22.

plined mind is a second-best substitute for "true wisdom." On the other hand, they do not seem to be the whole of virtue either. At any rate, it seems to many that a truly good person will be both conscientious and benevolent, where the latter includes kindness, generosity, compassion, and sympathy.

Kant apparently denied this, maintaining that only acts done from duty have "moral worth." I understand him to mean that only when an agent conscientiously follows the Supreme Principle of Morality will his actions reflect *moral* credit upon him. Kant allowed that other virtues are desirable and should be encouraged, but one form of conscientiousness (Kant called it "good will") is of incomparably higher worth than other virtues and is the source of all *moral* worth.

This view of moral worth is obviously connected with Kant's theory of freedom and the autonomy of reason. The very possibility of rationality and personality depends, for Kant, upon the possibility of acting from duty. Setting aside the metaphysical aspects of Kant's theory, there are still arguments for his theory of moral worth. Sympathy, kindness, and compassion can lead a person to do what *he* takes to be morally wrong. These sentiments may on occasion constitute inclinations contrary to the promptings of duty, opposing one's opinion about what one should do. "Good will," on the other hand, never tempts a person to act contrary to what he takes to be morally required of him. On Kant's view, there is a single decision procedure for determining what is morally permissible and what is not, and the Supreme Principle of Morality directs one to avoid actions that are not permissible according to this procedure. "Good will" consists in the conscientious commitment to following this principle. "Good will" thus turns out to be a commitment to doing what, on moral grounds, one should do. Nothing else is needed. Moreover, any other commitment or sentiment that could possibly conflict with the promptings of "good will" must be subordinated to it.

If one accepts Kant's "single principle" moral theory, the case for the primacy of "good will" among the virtues is strong. There is good reason, however, to reject Kant's principle. The decision procedure he proposes, in all of its several formulations, is notoriously unsatisfactory. For the reasons advanced in the last section, morevoer, there is no hope of discovering a single procedure for making all such decisions. The character that can be relied upon to do what morally should be done is properly conceived as a complex of traits that will include, among other things, the virtues that are forms of conscientiousness—honesty, fairness, etc.—and also good judgment. Any one of these virtues may often lead to wrong action if it is not properly balanced by other traits.

It is possible, of course, to talk about a commitment to do what the morally good person would do, or a commitment to do what, all things considered, one should do. In situations in which it is clear what one should do, but one is tempted to do something else, such a commitment will stand one in good stead. A firm determination to do what one morally should do, however, will not result generally in one's actually doing what one should do unless it is accompanied by a sensitivity to an enormous range of considerations that are relevant to determining what one should do, together with the experience and the intelligence to deal with these factors. To understand what it is to be a good person, one does best to focus upon the elements of the complex.

A similar point can be made about intellectual character. One might say that an unwavering determination to get to the bottom of things is the chief virtue of an inquirer. Such a commitment, however, is of little avail in finding the truth unless it is accompanied by a great many other things: knowledge, experience, discipline, ingenuity, and skill. If one wishes to understand what a good inquirer is, one must attend to this complex of qualities and traits and their interrelations. Moral character, like intellectual character, is a system made up of a number of traits and skills in a delicate structure.

If we take it as established that the virtues that are forms of conscientiousness are an indispensable part of personal merit, the question remains whether these virtues are not somehow more important or valuable than other kinds of virtues. Kant maintained that a "good will" is the only thing that is unconditionally good, since no matter how one's efforts turn out, if conscientiousness about duty is one's motive, there is always something good to be said for the action and the agent—one meant well. Conscientiousness, however, either in the form of "good will" or in the form of honesty, fairness, etc., is not unique in this respect. If someone acts from kindness, then no matter what is wrong with his so doing or how it turns out, there is something good to be said for him—he was trying to be kind.

Prichard suggested that "the sense of obligation," although important, is not a major factor in the lives of those who are most interesting and admirable. Whether one agrees or disagrees with this view depends upon whom one regards as "most interesting and admirable." Abraham Lincoln seems to me an absolutely clear and uncontroversial counterexample to Prichard's claim. The important point, however, is that judgments about which virtues are most valuable and what lives are most interesting and admirable are highly idiosyncratic.

I conclude that the virtues that are forms of conscientiousness are reasonably regarded as traits necessary in a truly good person, though it is reasonable to expect that other sorts of virtues are required too. The question of which virtues are most important for a good person seems to me to deserve the same sort of answer as the question of which organs of the body are most important for life and health. Personal merit, like good health, requires the proper functioning of many different elements. Good judgment and the virtues that are forms of conscientiousness are an indispensable part of personal merit.

I have tried to draw up a brief in defense of virtues that are forms of conscientiousness, particularly in response to the charge that such traits involve attitudes that are not altogether enlightened and reasonable. These virtues are, I have maintained, commitments to forms of behavior that we, as a community, reasonably require of one another. Such commitments are a part—though only a part—of the elaborate psychological and intellectual equipment required for human reasonableness and goodness.

V

Benevolence

By benevolence I understand a genus or family of virtues of which kindness, generosity, humaneness, and compassion are (overlapping) species or forms. All of these virtues, at least in their primary manifestations, involve a direct concern for the happiness and well-being of others—or, as I shall say, for the *good* of others. This concern manifests itself both in feelings and in actions. It is similar in important respects to the concern for the good of another that is characteristic of the best sort of affection and friendship.

Aristotle in discussing *philia* said: "[The good man] is related to his friend as to himself (for his friend is another self)."[1] Bishop Butler used the same analogy in discussing compassion. "When we rejoice in the prosperity of others, and compassionate their distress, we, as it were, substitute them for ourselves, their interest for our own."[2]

In all of these things—benevolence, affection, and friendship—there is a certain direct concern for another's good that

1. *Nicomachean Ethics*, IX, 4, 1166a30–31.
2. Joseph Butler, *Fifteen Sermons Preached at Rolls Chapel*, Sermon V, Paragraph (1) (London: G. Bell, 1914), p. 83.

is like an individual's concern for his own good. Thus, one tends to feel about the good and ill fortune of one's friends as one feels about one's own—rejoicing, grieving, feeling proud or ashamed as the circumstances warrant. One also tends to act in ways that promote a friend's good just as one acts to promote one's own good. Selfishness and jealousy, of course, sometimes intrude in the relationships of lovers and friends and compete with this tendency to promote each others' good.

One may treat someone with kindness and compassion without necessarily feeling any affection for him. One can act and feel toward strangers in ways that are fully characteristic of kindness, compassion, and generosity. What *is* common to both affection *and* primary benevolence is that they involve a direct concern for the good—that is, the happiness and well-being—of another person. The person is, for the agent, another self.

Kindness, generosity, and compassion are not forms of conscientiousness, although it is sometimes difficult to distinguish them from conscientiousness. We are morally required to refrain from harming people in certain ways, and there are duties to help people in certain circumstances. Often, the actions required of us in such cases are also actions that kindness or compassion would incline us to undertake. Thus, someone who is *both* conscientious about such duties *and* benevolent is doubly motivated in such situations to promote another's good. Moreover, the *scope* of duties to help others and duties to refrain from harming them is often difficult to determine. Apart from special relationships to others—family members, neighbors, colleagues, etc.—we are normally required to help any person in distress when we can do so easily. Generally, apart from special relationships, we are not required to help others at huge costs to ourselves. Between these extremes, however, lies a wide range of cases in which it is unclear whether one is required to help or not, whether the person in distress can claim one's aid as his right, whether he is wronged if aid is withheld. When a person who is both conscientious and benevolent helps another in such circumstances, it is often not clear to anyone, including the agent, whether he is morally required to do so. Despite this blurring and overlapping, the two sorts of virtues—forms of conscientiousness and forms of benevolence—can be distinguished. A benevolent person is not concerned merely about avoiding certain forms of behavior that he regards as wrong; he is directly concerned for the good of other people.

If morality is conceived, after the manner of Kant, as consisting exclusively in the conscientious observance of rules or laws requiring people to behave in certain ways, then benevolence will seem, at best, a kind of second-rate moral virtue, to be encouraged because the behavior characteristic of it often coincides with what the rules prescribe. This view, however, does not do justice to the value we place upon kindness, compassion, and generosity. We believe that however conscientious someone might be, if he were altogether lacking these virtues that are forms of benevolence, he would be seriously defective as a human being. We must ask what basis there is for this belief.

Periodically, often in reaction to strongly legalistic conceptions of morality, it is maintained that love and benevolence are morally superior to conscientiousness. According to the New Testament, the two great commandments enjoin us to love God and to love our neighbors as ourselves. Kant insisted, however, that it is not possible to feel, on command, affection for someone. Since we cannot love someone *at will*, it seems pointless to command us to love. The commandment to love one's neighbors, according to Kant, should be understood as the command to practice all duties toward one's neighbors. Kant called this "practical love." The moral incentive to follow such commands, on this view, is respect for law rather than love for one's neighbors.[3]

We are morally required to refrain from harming others in certain situations, and sometimes we do wrong if we fail to aid people who need help. Benevolence, in its various forms, will

---

3. *Critique of Practical Reason*, L. W. Beck, trans. (Indianapolis and New York: Liberal Arts Press, 1956), p. 86.

often lead an individual to act in ways that coincide with the behavior prescribed by these requirements, so that conscientiousness about these duties and benevolence generally result in the same action *in these cases.* In other sorts of cases, the promptings of benevolence may conflict with duties. Some meritorious actions that are fully characteristic of forms of benevolence, moreover, are *actions that are not morally required of us.*

In order to separate benevolence from conscientiousness and to discover the basis of the peculiar merit of the former, I will examine certain of these actions that are not morally required but that are fully characteristic of virtues that are forms of benevolence. If such actions are so valuable and desirable that they reflect credit upon the agent as a human being, why are these actions not required of us? If reasons can be found why it is better that such actions not be generally required of us, then these, together with an account of why those virtues are valued, should contribute to an understanding of both conscientiousness and benevolence.

Let us simplify matters to begin with by restricting the discussion to a single form of benevolence. Generosity is particularly concerned with actions that are not required of us, and it is not difficult to see the similarities and differences between generosity and other forms of benevolence. For these reasons I will begin with generosity. After a discussion of what generosity is, I take up the questions of how it might be argued that generosity is a virtue and why it would be undesirable to require people always to act as a generous person would act.

1. *Economic Generosity*

Generosity is concerned with giving, and different kinds of generosity can be distinguished according to the kind of things given. Aristotle said that generosity (*eleutheriotēs*) has to do with giving and taking of things whose value is measured in money.[4] There is a virtue called generosity, the actions fully characteristic

4. *Nicomachean Ethics*, IV, 1, 1119b21–27.

of which are meritorious, which has to do with freely giving things that have a *market value*—freely giving goods and services of a type that normally are exchanged on the open market. This sort of generosity I call "economic generosity" to distinguish it from other varieties. One can be generous in the judgments one makes about the merits and demerits of others, and one can be generous in forgiving those who trespass against one. "Generous-mindedness" and "generous-heartedness," as these other kinds of generosity might be called, do not involve being generous with things whose value is measured in money. These are like economic generosity in certain ways, but they also differ in important respects, as I shall try subsequently to show. Unless otherwise indicated, however, by generosity I mean economic generosity.

A generous person is one who has a certain attitude toward his own things, the value of which is measured in money, and who also has a certain attitude toward other people. Generosity, like other forms of benevolence, in its primary occurrence, involves as one of its constituents a concern for the happiness and well-being of others. The actions fully characteristic of generosity have as their goal promoting someone else's well-being, comfort, happiness, or pleasure—someone else's good. In *primary generosity*, the agent is concerned directly about the good of another. Thus, an action fully characteristic of generosity might be done to please someone or to help someone, with no further end in view beyond pleasing or helping. "I just wanted to do something nice for them" or "I just wanted her to have it" are typical explanations of generous acts.

That an act fully characteristic of *the virtue*, generosity, is motivated in this way by a direct concern for the good of another is not immediately obvious, because we sometimes call giving "generous" and mean only that the giver is giving more than someone in his situation normally gives. Thus, the host is being generous with the mashed potatoes when he unthinkingly heaps unusually large portions on the plates. Or perhaps he does not do it unthinkingly. It might be that he is giving such generous portions because he wants to use up all the potatoes to prevent them from spoiling. Being generous in this way—giving a lot for reasons such as these—would not tend to show that the host is a *generous person*, even if he did so frequently. If we restrict ourselves to the kind of generous action that is fully characteristic of a generous person, then in every case, the agent's giving will be motivated by a direct concern for the good (in the broad sense) of another. I shall say in such cases that the agent intends to *benefit* the recipient.

There is a further complication. The virtue generosity, in its *primary occurrence*, I have said, involves a sort of direct concern for the good of others, as do other forms of benevolence. Someone who is deficient in such concern or who lacks it altogether might admire generous people for their generosity and want as far as he can to be like them. He might then want to do in certain situations what a generous person would do. Acting as a generous person would act because one regards generosity as a virtue and wants, therefore, to emulate the generous person is meritorious, and it reflects credit upon the agent. It is, however, a secondary sort of generosity. It depends, for its merit, upon the fact that primary generosity *is* a virtue and is thus a worthy ideal at which to aim. I will concentrate, therefore, upon primary generosity, which does involve a direct concern for the good of another. An account of why this is a virtue is easily extended to explain why a generous person is worthy of emulation.

A certain sort of attitude on the part of the agent toward what he gives is also a feature of actions fully characteristic of the virtue generosity. In acting generously, one must give something that one values—something that one, therefore, has some reason to keep rather than discard or abandon. If, for example, one is about to throw away an article of clothing, and on the way to the trash barrel one meets someone who would like to have it, it would not be *generous* of one to give it to him. What disqualifies such giving from being generous is neither the giver's motive nor the nature of what is given but rather the fact that the giver himself does not value the object enough. Similarly, when we do favors for one another, giving matches or coins for parking meters, often what is given is too insignificant for the giving of it to be generous. One may be being kind in giving things that one does not particularly value, but for the giving to be generous, one must value the thing given for some reason. I may have acquired a particularly repulsive piece of primitive art that I have no desire to keep. Still, I might generously give it to a museum if it were a valuable piece—one I could sell or exchange for something I really want. *How generous* one is being in giving something generally depends upon how much one values the thing given, how much one is giving up.

Usually, the giver must give in excess of what he is required to give by morality or custom, if his giving is to be generous. Where there exists a generally recognized moral obligation to give, or where giving is customary, then normally one's giving is not generous even though it is prompted by a direct concern for the good of the recipient. If one were certain of a more than ample and continuing supply of food, so that it would clearly be wrong not to give some food to a neighbor who would otherwise go hungry, giving the neighbor a portion of food would not be generous. Similarly, to give a person a gift when one is expected to do so, because it is customary to exchange gifts (for example birthdays, Christmas, weddings, etc.), is normally not a matter of generosity, even though one aims to please the recipient. If one gives *more* than what is expected in such cases, then the giving might be generous. A generous person is one who exceeds normal expectations in giving, and one who gives no more than what is generally expected in the circumstances is not apt to be cited for generosity.

A special problem arises in cases of the following sort. Although it would clearly be wrong for a certain person *not* to give, he does not see this. Nevertheless, he does give on a generous impulse. Suppose, for example, that a certain person is a social Darwinist, convinced that it is wrong to give the necessities of life to people in need, because this enables the weak to survive, thus weakening the species. She encounters a starving family, and, touched by their plight, she provides food for them, though not without a twinge of social Darwinist guilt. Assuming that what she gives is not insignificant to her, but that it is no more than what the family needs to keep them alive, is her giving generous? On the one hand, she is really doing no more than the minimum required of her by the duty to help people in distress, and this makes one hesitate to say that she is being generous. On the other hand, *she* does not recognize any moral obligation here, and it is the kind and generous side of her nature that overcomes her cruel principles and leads her to give. This seems to support the view that she is being generous.

An act fully characteristic of generosity will normally have the following features.

(1) The agent, because of his direct concern for the good of the recipient, gives something with the intention of benefiting the recipient.

(2) The agent gives up something of his that has a market value and that he has some reason to value and, therefore, to keep.

(3) The agent gives more than one is generally expected, because of moral requirements or custom, to give in such circumstances.

In normal cases, an act that meets these three conditions will be a generous act, and a generous act will have these three features. There are, however, abnormal cases—cases in which the agent has, concerning the circumstances mentioned in the three conditions, a false belief or an unusual or eccentric attitude. The case of the social Darwinist is such a case. She thinks she is morally required *not* to give, when in fact she is required to give. If one accepts *her* view of the situation, her act is generous. In fact, however, the third condition is not satisfied. In another sort of abnormal case, the agent values what he gives, but in fact the gift is utterly worthless—it is literally trash. Here it is not clear that the second condition is fulfilled, but from the agent's odd point of view, the act is generous. The very rich often give to charity sums of money that are large in comparison with what others give, and their gifts seem generous. These sums, however, which are substantial, may be relatively insignificant to the donors, and one may wonder whether condition (2) is satisfied in such a case. Does the donor, who has so much, in fact have reason to value and keep what he gives, or is his "gift" analogous to an ordinary person's giving away a book of matches? In a rather different sort of case, someone might be convinced that he is morally required to give away nearly all he has to the poor. For this reason, he divests himself of a substantial fortune. In such cases, it may be that condition (1) is not satisfied. The agent believes, in effect, that condition (3) is not satisfied, since he believes that he is required to do this. These circumstances will make one hesitate to call his giving generous, although other features of the case incline one toward the view that he is being generous.

In these cases involving unusual beliefs or attitudes, one is pulled simultaneously in two different directions. The way the agent sees the situation and the way one expects him to see the situation diverge. Crucial conditions are satisfied from one way of regarding the case and unsatisfied from the other. It is not surprising that one is reluctant to say simply that the act is (or is not) fully characteristic of the virtue generosity. Any such statement must be qualified, and the actual consequences of the qualification may or may not be important, depending upon the case. Normally, of course, the agent's beliefs about the features in (1)–(3) will not be grossly mistaken nor will his attitudes toward those things be unusual or eccentric. In such cases, if the three conditions are satisfied, the act is unqualifiedly generous, and vice versa.

A generous person is one who has a tendency to perform actions that meet these conditions. The stronger the tendency, the more generous the person.

2. Generous-Mindedness

The conditions in the preceding section are meant as an account of actions that are fully characteristic of *economic generosity*—generosity that involves giving things whose value is measured in money. Another kind of generosity, however, has to do with making judgments about the merits and failings of other people. This too is a virtue, which sometimes is called *generous-mindedness*. [5] I will try briefly to indicate some similarities and differences between this virtue and economic generosity.

Generous-mindedness is shown by seeing someone else's merit (technical, moral, etc.) in cases where it is difficult to see because the facts of the case admit of other, not unreasonable interpretations, or because the situation is complex and the merit is not immediately apparent. Generous-mindedness is also shown by seeing that a derogatory judgment is not called for in cases where the facts might not unreasonably be taken to indicate a derogatory judgment. Many of us actually dislike to find that others are as good or better than we are, so that we have some desire to find grounds for derogatory judgments. It is plausible to think that people of otherwise fair judgment are sometimes led to think less well of others than they should because they do not want to think well of them or because they want to think ill of them. They do not purposely close their eyes to merit; rather because they do not wish to find it, they do not try hard enough to find it. This may involve a certain amount of self-deception, but I suspect that in many cases the matter is more straightforward. If someone wants to find another inferior to himself in some respect, then where he sees some (prima facie) grounds for such a judgment, he is apt to be quick to seize upon it and regard the matter as settled. A generous-minded person is one who wants to think well of other people, so that in such cases he will look and find the merit that might otherwise go overlooked. Of course, it is possible to be too generous-minded—to overlook demerit because one does not want to find it.

If someone exhibits generous-mindedness in his judgment on a particular occasion, his act of judgment will not fulfill the conditions for an act of economic generosity. It will have features,

5. I am indebted to David Shwayder for bringing this topic to my attention.

however, that can be seen as analogous to the features characteristic of economic generosity. If an individual is well-disposed
toward other people, then besides wanting to benefit them by
giving them things, he will wish them well. He will tend to want
their undertakings to succeed and to reflect well on them. If he
wants to think well of others, he will be apt to look harder for merit,
and he will, therefore, be more likely to find it. Generous-
mindedness seems properly regarded as a manifestation of good
will toward others that shows a direct concern for the well-being
of others.

Economic generosity generally involves giving more than is
required or customary, and there is a counterpart to this in
generous-mindedness. The generous-minded person sees merit
where a competent evaluator might miss it, where it would be
reasonable (though incorrect) to find that there is no such merit.
In this way, one might say that generous-mindedness leads a
person to go beyond what is required of an evaluator. It is less
clear whether there is with generous-mindedness a counterpart of
the second condition for primary generosity—whether there is
something of value to the agent that he gives up in being
generous-minded. Two things suggest themselves for this role.
One would expect that a generous-minded person will make a
greater effort to find merit or to put a not unfavorable construc-
tion on facts that look bad, thus giving up time and effort. Secondly, in searching for the most favorable interpretation possible,
a person, if he succeeds, must sometimes thereby forego the
generally congenial thought that he is better than or as good as
another. No doubt, a generous-minded person does not always
expend more time and energy in making an assessment than he
would if he were not generous-minded. Moreover, the generous-
minded person is no doubt less likely than most to enjoy thinking
himself better than others. It does seem that the parallels are not
exact, and that "generosity" is used metaphorically in generous-
mindedness.

For generous-mindedness not to distort one's judgment—for it
not to lead one to incorrect evaluations—an individual must be a

competent evaluator and be conscientious about reaching a correct judgment. Also, it does seem that if one has sufficiently good judgment and is sufficiently concerned to make the right judgment, then this by itself should lead one to see merit when it is present just as well as would the desire *to find merit.* The strong desire to make favorable judgments, moreover, *may* distort one's judgment. It may lead one to overlook defects and to find merit where it is not. A strong desire to make *the correct evaluation* cannot distort one's judgment in this way. Generous-mindedness should not be regarded as a primary virtue of evaluators. It can counteract an inclination to build oneself up by tearing others down, but so too can a strong desire to evaluate correctly. Generous-mindedness is a manifestation of the sort of concern for others that is characteristic of all forms of benevolence. It derives the greatest part of its merit from this concern.

3. *Generosity as a Mean*

Aristotle conceived of "moral virtues" as "means" with respect to certain feelings or actions. Thus, the virtue V, conceived as a mean with respect to feeling f, would be the tendency to experience f in the right degree, neither too much nor too little. The tendency to experience f too strongly would be a vice, K, and the tendency to feel f too little would be a different vice, K'. It is useful to attempt to apply this model to the concept of economic generosity sketched by conditions (1)–(3) in section 1 of this chapter. Those conditions, once again, are:

(1) The agent, because of his direct concern for the good of the recipient, gives something with the intention of benefiting the recipient.

(2) The agent gives up something of his that has a market value and that he has some reason to value and, therefore, to keep.

(3) The agent gives more than one is generally expected, because of moral requirements or custom, to give in such circumstances.

An act that is fully characteristic of economic generosity re-flects credit upon the agent. Because condition (3) must be fulfil-led for an act to be unqualifiedly generous, however, refraining from such an act is not apt to be wrong. Normally, we have indefinitely many opportunities to act generously. We are sur-rounded by other people we could benefit by giving things, people to whom we are not required to give. The omission of any particular one of these actions will not by itself be apt to reflect badly upon a person. Never acting generously, however, is symp-tomatic of some vice incompatible with generosity.

We tend to think of stinginess or meanness as *the* vice that is the opposite of the virtue generosity, but in fact meanness is not the only vice incompatible with generosity. This sort of meanness involves an *excessive* concern with one's own things. Because of this, a mean person is disinclined to give up things he values, and so he is disinclined to make the sort of sacrifice required by the third condition for acting generously. Meanness, then, is a trait that can be seen in someone's being so attached to what is his that he never acts generously. The same excessive concern for one's things, however, might manifest itself in other ways. It might, for example, lead someone to default on his debts, or it might lead him to sacrifice his own happiness. The *pleonexia* (graspingness, greed) of Aristotle's unjust man is related to the stingy person's excessive desire to keep what is his. Anyone who, because of his desire to get and keep things, never acts gener-ously, fails consistently in his obligations, or sacrifices his own happiness could properly be said to be excessively concerned with his belongings. Such excessive concern, called meanness or stin-giness, is incompatible with generosity.

Other traits incompatible with generosity but distinguishable from meanness involve a lack of concern for the happiness and well-being of others. A person might be so self-absorbed, so cold, or so hostile to other people that he would have little inclination to do things for their benefit. Because (1) is a necessary condition for an act's being (unqualifiedly) generous, such people would be unlikely to act generously.

Benevolence

These points suggest that the virtue generosity is the Aristotelian mean with respect to (i) concern for one's own things that have a market value—that is, the desire to keep these and preserve them and (ii) concern for the good of others.[6] To the extent that the Aristotelian model is appropriate, excessess and deficiencies of these concerns will be constitutive of vices that are incompatible with generosity. An *excessive* concern with one's own possessions, etc., together with too little concern for the well-being of others, does constitute the vice meanness or stinginess. On the other hand, too little concern with one's possessions—a lack of concern approaching indifference—would tend to diminish one's generosity. One is not being generous if one is indifferent to what one gives away. Hence, generosity does involve a mean between too much and too little concern for one's possessions, etc. At the same time, too little concern for the well-being and happiness of others, which might be simply indifference or active dislike of others, is also incompatible with generosity. Depending upon the circumstances, this deficiency of concern might be callous indifference, it might be selfishness if the indifference were due to a preoccupation with one's own concerns, or it might be general hostility (misanthropy) or malevolence if it were due to active dislike of others. A deficiency of concern for others, then, is incompatible with generosity.

It is less clear, however, what an excess of concern for the good of others would be and whether such an excess would be incompatible with generosity. Someone might give away so much of his time, energy, and possessions that he is unable to meet his own needs and responsibilities. Such behavior might be due, however, to irresponsibility rather than unusual concern for the good of another. That is, the agent may simply fail to take thought about his future needs and responsibilities. It may be, too, that

6. Although I am using Aristotle's notion of "a mean" here, I am not expounding his account of *eleutheriotēs* as a mean. The idea that generosity involves neither too much nor too little concern to get and keep goods is not foreign to Aristotle, but the notion that it also involves a concern for the good of others is un-Aristotelian.

this is a mistake in judgment; he did take thought but he underes-
timated what he would need. It would be necessary to say a great
deal to describe convincingly a person who is excessively concerned for the good of others. Such a person would take care of
himself, his possessions, and his obligations, showing a normal
degree of concern for such things, except in situations in which
he thought he could promote the good of someone else. Then, in
pursuing this course, he would neglect these other things, though
with some regret. Even if there is such a thing as this sort of
excessive concern for the good of others, however, this does not
constitute a character trait *incompatible with generosity*. Rather,
insofar as this sort of excessive concern led one to give away too
much of one's time, energy, and possessions, it seems quite properly described as an excess of generosity—being generous to a
fault. Such a character trait is not quite a vice incompatible with
generosity. Such a person would frequently do just what a generous person would do. His behavior, which exhibits an excess of
generosity, however, can be faulted. Of such excessively generous acts, something good can be said and something bad can be
said. This is characteristic of other kinds of virtues-in-excess—
being too honest, being honest to a fault, for example.

Why is it that an excess of concern for others does not constitute a vice that is an opposite of generosity in the way that a
deficiency of such concern does, or in the way that an excess of
concern for one's possessions does? An explanatory hypothesis is
that a virtue is prized because it plays a certain role in human life;
it has one or more useful functions. An excess of concern for the
good of another may have bad effects—this is what makes it
excessive. These bad effects, however, do not thwart the
functions of the virtue. They do not prevent it from playing its
characteristic role. Before we can consider the plausibility of this
hypothesis in the present case, however, we must discover the
functions of generosity.

It is not completely accurate, then, to say that the virtue
generosity involves a mean between too much and too little concern for the good of others, where the extremes of the concern

(excess and deficiency) each constitute a vicious character trait incompatible with generosity. Generosity does, nonetheless, involve the proper degree of concern for one's possessions, etc.—being neither too much nor too little concerned for them, and it involves also a certain concern for the good of others. The latter concern, however, insofar as it is involved in generosity, does not fit perfectly the virtue-as-mean model, since an excess of concern is not something other than generosity.

A generous person is one who, because of his concern for the good of others and because he is neither too much nor too little concerned about his possessions, is disposed to act in ways that fulfill the conditions for an act fully characteristic of generosity, conditions (1)–(3) above. How frequently would a generous person be expected to act in these ways and toward whom? As a rule, we regard someone as a generous person only when he acts generously more frequently and to a greater degree than most people do. A generous person is one who is inclined to act generously to a noteworthy extent. Most of us are neither generous enough to count as generous persons nor ungenerous enough to possess one of the vices incompatible with generosity. There would seem to be no reason why a generous person *must* care about the good of *every* human being. The beneficiaries of one's generosity might be restricted to a circle of friends. Still, an individual who is "a friend of man," whose concern extends potentially to all whom he encounters, has a wider scope for his generosity. His generosity is not limited to a certain group of people, and thus he is apt to be more generous than someone whose generosity is limited.

Kindness and compassion are less complex traits than generosity. Like generosity, they are "other regarding" virtues. That is, they involve in their primary occurrence a direct concern for the good of others. A person's kindness may manifest itself in generous acts, but it may also manifest itself in acts that do not involve giving anything with a value measured in money. Kindness consists simply in a certain sort of direct concern for the happiness and well-being of others, together with a sensitivity to the situation of other people. Kind people are not only prone to benefit other people, but they are also quick to see *how* they might benefit them. What might be called the psychological structure of the character trait kindness is less complex than that of generosity. The latter involves the tendency to serve others' good in ways many people find difficult, because they find it difficult to part with things that have monetary value. Thus generosity involves the right degree of concern about such things—neither too much nor too little. There is no counterpart to this with kindness. Thus, it is possible for a person to be a kind person without being a generous person. Someone who was raised in conditions of penury might become so conditioned that even when he has enough money, he finds it difficult to part with any. Such a person might be kind and compassionate without being generous.

Compassion, according to the *Oxford English Dictionary*, is "the feeling or emotion when a person is moved by the suffering or distress of another and by the desire to relieve it." A compassionate person is one who has a tendency to feel and respond in this way to the misfortunes of others. Someone may have this tendency without being particularly concerned to benefit people who are not in difficulty. It is possible, then, for someone to be a compassionate person without being in any noteworthy degree a kind or generous person.

These traits that are forms of benevolence, then, tend to overlap. It is possible, though, to have certain of these traits without the others. They are in this sense distinct.

4. *Obligations to Help Others*

The question to be answered is: wherein lies the merit of generosity? Why do we regard an act that satisfies conditions (1)–(3) as an act having merit, an act that reflects credit upon the agent? It might seem that this is an easy question to answer. Generous people serve human needs and interests in fairly obvious ways, and the rationale for regarding generosity as a virtue is to be found here. If this answer is accepted, however, it leads to another question, the answer to which is by no means obvious.

Because of condition (3) for a generous act, there is a contrast between acts of giving that are generous and acts of giving that are expected of us because of custom or moral obligation. If generous acts have merit, however, because they tend to serve human needs and interests in important ways, why do we not raise our expectations? Why do we not require generosity of one another, as we require the forms of behavior characteristic of honesty, etc? If a reasonable explanation of the merit of *free* giving as opposed to *obligatory* giving can be found, it should shed light upon both generosity and obligations to give to others. There are, of course, such obligations, but when an act of giving is required in this way, then it is unlikely to qualify as generous, unless the giving in some respect exceeds what is required.

If philosophical ethics is thought to be concerned exclusively with moral rules or laws and the actions they require of us, then generosity is apt to be left out of account altogether. Some who do so conceive of ethics admit that there are acts of supererogation—acts that are morally praiseworthy, though not required by rules—but these are apt to be thought of as extraordinary exhibitions of heroism or saintliness.[7] That there are meritorious actions such as generous acts which are neither extraordinary nor required needs to be noted and explained.

It is necessary first to examine a kind of giving that *is* required of us in order to understand why such giving should be required. The sort of obligatory giving I have in mind is not that involved in exchanges, where one is required to reciprocate, nor is it the sort of giving that might be required by a person's special relationship to another (parent, child, etc.). I am thinking, rather, of the sort of giving that is sometimes required of us when another person—any person—is in need of help and we are in a position to help. The aid we might give in such cases *sometimes* involves giving something whose value is measured in money, although this is not always the case. In all of these cases, kindness, compassion, or generosity might move a person to give aid, but we do not

7. For an incisive discussion of this topic, see Joel Feinberg, "Supererogation and Rules," *International Journal of Ethics*, 71 (1961), 276–288.

depend entirely upon such sentiments. We *require* one another to render aid in certain circumstances.

It is not difficult to provide a rationale for the obligation to render aid—that is, to show the reasonableness of the requirement. It is evident that each of us is likely to be better off if everyone is prepared to render aid, when he can do so easily, to a person who is in difficulty, than we would be if a substantial number of people were not so prepared. For every such service performed, there will be a loss to the agent (his sacrifice) and a gain to the person helped. In each case, however, the loss will be small in comparison to the gain, unless the agent fails to bring about the benefits he intends. Thus, it is possible to argue that the benefits of such a requirement greatly outweigh the inconveniences, even though attempts to render aid sometimes fail. No individual under such a practice is guaranteed that *his* benefits from the aid of others will exceed his inconvenience in rendering aid to others. It may turn out that his difficulties were few and small and the services required of him many. It is not prudent, however, for anyone to assume that he will not need help, any more than it is prudent for him to trust that his home will not burn down. Someone who at the end of his life found that the burden of helping others had been for him greater than the benefits he had received from others under the practice could regard his net loss as the reasonable price he had paid for insurance against the possibility of being in urgent need himself. Security is an additional benefit of the existence of the obligation to render aid.[8]

8. John Rawls advances similar arguments for "the duty of mutual aid" and adds, "The primary value of the principle [requiring mutual aid] is not measured by the help we actually receive but rather by the sense of confidence and trust in other men's good intentions and the knowledge that they are there if we need them. . . . Once we try to picture the life of a society in which no one had the slightest desire to act on these duties, we see that it would express an indifference if not disdain for human beings that would make a sense of our own worth impossible" (A *Theory of Justice*, p. 339). It seems to me, however, that it is a certain *lack* of concern, a certain indifference, if not disdain, for other human beings that makes such a *duty* necessary—which makes it necessary for

Benevolence

The foregoing can be taken as an argument for the desirability of there being such a practice as the obligation to render aid. It is also an argument for the reasonableness of the requirement that we aid one another where we can do so easily. Thus, someone might render aid in such circumstances because he is conscientious about this obligation, even though he is not moved by feelings of sympathy and compassion. Often, there is reason to suppose that an agent is influenced by both sorts of motives in helping a person in need.

In cases where it is in an agent's power to help another person in need, but where the sacrifice this entails for the agent is *not* small, the agent is not required to perform that service by the obligation to render aid. No one, for example, would suggest that Sidney Carton in A *Tale of Two Cities* was morally required to take the place of Charles Darnay under the blade of the guillotine, although Carton thereby rendered great service to Darnay and his family, a service that no one else could have rendered. Of course, Carton's sacrifice would not properly be characterized as "generous"—at least, this does not seem the right word. Carton did not give up something whose value is measured in money. In cases where the agent's sacrifice is not required by the obligation to render aid, and where he *does* give up something that has a market value, then his action may be generous, if his motive in giving is the right one.

Suppose, as is *not* the case, that people generally felt that on moral grounds they are required to help people in need of help, regardless of the cost to themselves. Let us call this imaginary requirement the Obligation of Service, and ask whether it would

---

us to *require* of one another such aid. If one could count upon everyone's benevolence toward everyone else, such a requirement would be superfluous. Given the degree of indifference that does exist, this duty does tend to promote confidence and trust as Rawls says. The existence of the duty, moreover, is an affirmation that people do matter. The knowledge that others have a benevolent concern for our good, however, is *more* efficacious in supporting our sense of our own worth than is the knowledge that others are conscientious about their duty to aid us. So I maintain, at any rate, in the last section of this chapter.

be desirable for there to be such an obligation. If there were such an obligation and if people were sufficiently conscientious about it, then people generally would make more and greater sacrifices than they do now. Of course, people would also be more apt to receive help from others. Life would be very different from what it is now if people took seriously such an Obligation of Service, and it is hard to know how things would seem to us if we lived this way. Still, it is doubtful that it would be desirable for there to be such a general obligation. If we consider the services that would be required if there were such an obligation, which are not already required by the existing obligation to render aid, there is no reason to suppose that the benefits of these would outweigh the burdens they would impose. One could not argue for the reasonableness of such a requirement in the way that one can argue for the reasonableness of the obligation to render aid.

Even supposing that this imaginary Obligation of Service were limited so that people are required to help those who need help only where the cost to the agent does not exceed the value of the service performed, the desirability of such an Obligation of Limited Service is doubtful. This limited obligation would require us to do things we are not now required to do. These additional things we would be required to do would be difficult things. We would sometimes be required to take upon ourselves substantial misfortunes. One might regard this as the cost of insurance against being in need of help oneself—insurance covering contingencies presently not covered. This, however, is very expensive insurance. It is doubtful whether there is a case of this sort for having an Obligation of Limited Service *rather than* the existing obligation to render aid when one can do so easily.

As the cost to the agent approaches the value of the service performed, it becomes increasingly odd to *require* the agent to help a person in need. This becomes odd because it seems in a certain way objectionably arbitrary. We are all more or less accustomed to the fact that we are apt to suffer misfortunes. Why should A, simply because he is in a position to alleviate *B*'s misfortune, be *required* to take upon himself a misfortune as serious or almost as serious as *B*'s? Why not let these misfortunes fall as they may, rather than require someone, who has the bad luck to be able to help, in effect to shoulder the misfortune that has befallen another? The following example is extreme, but the oddness of the requirement is very clear. If *B* desperately needed an immediate transfusion of five quarts of blood, and *A* was the only person available of the right blood type, then, other things being equal, the Obligation of Limited Service would require *A* to bleed to death to save *B*. In such a situation, of course, someone benefits from the Obligation of Limited Service—the individual needing the transfusion. In such a case, someone will die. Why should someone *be required* to take such a sacrifice upon himself? Is the recipient of the massive blood transfusion then required by the Obligation of Limited Service to return the blood to the donor in order to save the donor's life? If he is, then this seems silly. If he is not, then it seems arbitrary.

I conclude that there is reason to think it desirable that people recognize the obligation to render aid—the requirement that we render aid to other people when we can do so easily. In fact, we do require this of one another, and we do so reasonably. On the other hand, it appears that it would not be desirable for there to be a general obligation to help others no matter what the cost or a general obligation to help others unless the cost to the agent exceeds the value of the benefit rendered. Even this latter Obligation of Limited Service would be too much to require of one another.

5. *Some Merits of Generosity*

Of particular interest are the actions that are *not* required of us as things stand now but that would be required of us if there were an Obligation of Service or an Obligation of Limited Service. It would be characteristic of a kind, generous, or compassionate person to do such things. Where the service performed involved giving something having a market value, such actions, done from a direct concern for the recipient's good, would be fully characteristic of the virtue generosity. Not all generous acts, of course, belong to this class. Generosity and kindness can be exhibited toward people who are not in trouble. This class of actions is interesting, however, because we have seen that there is not a case for generally requiring people to do such things, and there is reason to think that we should not require *all* such actions of one another. Yet when people do such things from a direct concern for the good of others, these actions reflect credit upon them as actions fully characteristic of such a virtue as generosity, compassion, or kindness. Why do we so honor, praise and encourage actions that we are not willing to require of people? With this particular problem in mind, I wish to pursue the question 'Why is generosity a virtue?'

The first thing that comes to mind in seeking an answer to this last question is the fact that generous people are at times extremely useful. Anyone who has ever badly needed help and who has received help through people's generosity will testify to the usefulness of generosity. It is one thing, however, to find people with a certain trait useful and to be glad that there are such people. It is quite another to regard that trait as a virtue. In need, we might find gullible people every bit as useful as generous ones, but this does not show that gullibility is a virtue.

One might expect that the more generous people there are in one's community, the better off one is apt to be. What, however, of the price one pays in sacrifices and efforts by being generous oneself? Since the sacrifices made by generous people are in some cases sacrifices that are not small, it is not clear that the benefits a generous person can expect to receive from the generosity of others will be sufficient to offset the burdens of his own generous sacrifices—even if everyone is generous. Of course, one might enjoy the generosity of others without being generous oneself, and one might well profit thereby. The same point can be made, however, about gullibility. If one is not gullible oneself and others are gullible, one can hope to profit by taking advantage of their gullibility. It is evidently a mistake to try in this way to explain why generosity is a virtue.

To assume that one can show that generosity is a virtue by

showing that the benefits of generous giving are greater than the sacrifices such giving entails puts the matter in the wrong light, and this is not only because that such benefits would outweigh the cost is doubtful. For one thing, this way of looking at the matter suggests that one's generous acts are to be viewed as one's contribution to a mutually beneficial practice of generous giving. This line of thought, however, suggests that if one benefits from the general practice, one should do one's part. In other words, if the practice is generally beneficial, fairness requires that one act generously oneself. In fact, however, because of condition (3) for a generous act, generosity normally has to do with giving beyond what is generally expected or required of us. In addition, there is reason to think that it is better that such giving not be generally required of us. Finally, because of condition (1) for a generous act, such acts are motivated by a concern for the good of the recipient. To be motivated to give as one's fair share of the burden involved in a generally beneficial practice is different from being directly concerned about the recipient's good. Contractualist arguments and their near relatives are apt for showing the reasonableness of moral requirements, but since our task is to explain why generosity is a virtue, we do not want to show that we are required to act as a generous person acts.

Generous people give freely, willingly, because of their concern for the good of the recipients. If a generous person succeeds in benefiting another by his generosity, he has completed a project freely undertaken and achieved a result that he desires for its own sake. His success is apt to be for him a source of joy and satisfaction.[9] A generous person, then, is not to be seen as reluctantly making burdensome sacrifices. He gives freely, wanting to give, with no practice in the background that requires such giving. For the giver, as for the recipient, the benefits may well outweigh the burdens.

Once we abandon the idea that generosity can be shown to be a beneficial *practice* like promising, then it becomes clear that

9.   This point is stressed by Lester Hunt in "Generosity," *American Philosophical Quarterly*, 12 (1975), 235–244.

generosity is generally beneficial—that is, the more generous people there are, the better. In fact, if everyone were generous, then we would have, to a certain extent, the benefits that would attend an Obligation of Service without the disadvantages such an obligation would have—the diminution of freedom, the onerousness of making large sacrifices one is disinclined to make, and the arbitrariness of requiring people in effect to take upon themselves the misfortunes of others. The more generous people there are, the more apt one is to be the beneficiary of someone's generosity, though, of course, one could not count upon always receiving aid through people's generosity in the way that one could if everyone were very conscientious about an Obligation of Service.

Again, it might be argued that the more gullible people there are, the more apt one is to be able to benefit from people's gullibility. It is apparent, though, that gullibility is far more apt to be seriously disadvantageous to its possessor than generosity. As long as a gullible person is undeceived, he may be unperturbed by the fact that others are taking advantage of him, but when he tries to sell his uranium stock or paint "his" Brooklyn Bridge, he is bound to be disappointed. Moreover, it is disadvantageous to us in other ways if many members of our community are easily fooled. Gullible people cannot be counted upon in certain situations, and thus they are less satisfactory partners in joint enterprises.

6. *Benevolence, Good Will, and Self-Respect*

So far, the benefits of generosity that have been enumerated are (1) the value and the benefit to the recipient of the thing given and (2) the satisfaction to the agent from completing a project freely undertaken that produces a result he desires for its own sake. It does appear that generosity is a valuable trait just in the light of these benefits, and it is evident that a similar account can be given of the value of other forms of benevolence such as compassion and kindness.

I do not think, though, that the fact that benevolence in its various forms has such benefits is sufficient by itself to explain why we regard them as virtues. With all respect to David Hume, the fact that a trait is generally useful and agreeable to the possessor and to others is not sufficient to make it a virtue. Amiability, cleanliness, and wit are beneficial in these ways, but these traits do not tend to make one a good person. In order for a trait to be a virtue, it must tend to foster good human life in extensive and fundamental ways. It must be the perfection of a tendency or capacity that connects and interlocks with a variety of human goods in such a way that its removal from our lives would endanger the whole structure. Honesty, fairness, courage, and restraint must exist to some extent in most human beings in order for community and rationality to be possible. A people who lacked these traits altogether could not lead the sort of life that is characteristically human. Cleanliness and amiability make life pleasant in certain respects, but certain peoples have gotten along without them for centuries. If the virtues were removed from the scene, however, human life—the form of life characteristic of our kind—would be impossible. How can generosity, compassion, and kindness be shown to be of this magnitude of importance?

There are further ways in which forms of benevolence are beneficial. The appropriate response of one who is the beneficiary of someone's kindness or generosity is gratitude. This sentiment involves good will toward the benefactor and a desire in some way to reciprocate. In this way, virtues that are forms of benevolence tend to foster good feelings based upon mutual good will. That this result is both useful and satisfying in a community is manifest.

It is ironic, though, that the reaction of the beneficiary of someone's kindness or generosity is sometimes the very opposite of good will. The recipient sometimes feels resentment and even hatred towards his benefactor. Emerson's explanation of this reaction is suggestive.

The law of benefits is a difficult channel, which requires careful sailing, or rude boats. It is not the office of a man to receive gifts. How dare you give them? We wish to be self-sustained. We do not quite forgive a giver. The hand that feeds us is in some danger of being bitten. We can receive anything from love, for that is a way of receiving it from ourselves; but not from anyone who assumes to bestow. We somehow hate the meat which we eat, because there seems something of degrading dependence in living by it.[10]

A kind and generous person often can avert such resentment or at least minimize it by tact. He must take care not to damage the self-esteem of a beneficiary by emphasizing the beneficiary's dependence. As Emerson suggests, the recipient of kindness may feel himself diminished by his position of dependence. If the benefactor gives the impression that *he* regards the recipient as inferior, if he is condescending, the beneficiary is apt to resent him. Emerson suggests that the giver can avoid this by making it clear that the paramount consideration for him is the good of the recipient. "We can receive anything from love," Emerson says, "for that is a way of receiving it from ourselves." The very fact of the benefactor's concern for the good of the recipient underlines the worth and importance of the beneficiary to the benefactor. The recipient, feeling diminished by his dependence, is reassured by a demonstration of concern *for him*, an affirmation that he matters. Such concern, of course, is an essential element in kindness, generosity, and compassion. Unfortunately, even if a kind and generous person is tactful and makes his motives absolutely clear, a beneficiary may still resent and hate him. Such a response reflects poorly on the beneficiary, however, and argues a defect in him. That such a reaction strikes us as perverse seems to me evidence that this sort of response, while not exactly rare, is not the usual one either.

The fact that acts fully characteristic of kindness, generosity, and compassion tend to support the self-esteem of those who are the beneficiaries of these actions is an extremely important one for explaining the merit of benevolence. A demonstration of con-

10. "Gifts," *The Complete Works of Ralph Waldo Emerson*, III (Boston and New York: Houghton, Mifflin, 1903), 162.

cern for the good of an individual shows him that he is important and enhances his sense of his own worth. John Rawls calls self-respect "perhaps the most important primary good." "Without it nothing may seem worth doing, or if some things have value for us, we lack the will to strive for them. All desire and activity become empty and vain, and we sink into apathy and cynicism."[11]

A morality that requires us to respect one another in certain ways, that forbids us to use one another as "means alone," fosters the idea that each of us is important and valuable. This is Rawls's point.[12]

Virtues that are forms of benevolence tend also to promote self-respect and to support the view that individual human beings are valuable and important. *One* of the benefits of the best sort of friendships is that the affection and esteem of others for an individual supports his view of his own importance and worth. Similarly, the concern shown for an individual by those who treat him with kindness, generosity, or compassion tends to support his self-esteem. This concern is most sorely missed when it is absent; the feeling that everyone around one is indifferent toward one is truly demoralizing.

These points suggest an explanation of why we feel that something important would be missing in someone who is conscientious about giving aid to others when it is required of him but who lacks the direct concern for the good of others that is necessary for the forms of (primary) benevolence. Such a person is concerned about the *form* of behavior, doing his part, etc. He shows respect for important and necessary ways of acting. He lacks a direct concern for the good of other people, however, which shows that he does not regard them as intrinsically important or valuable. Not caring about something, of course, is an immediate indication that one does not regard it as important or valuable. Since he lacks a sense of the importance, the worth, of

11. A *Theory of Justice*, p. 440.
12. Ibid., §§29, 67.

other people, it is hard to see how he could have a sense of his own worth as a person. One would think that he would realize that he is not all that different from other people. Some degree of benevolence, then, is an integral part of appreciating the value and importance of a person. A person who possessed the virtues that are forms of conscientiousness but who lacked all benevolence would be unable fully to appreciate the point of the requirements he respects. We reasonably require certain things of one another because these forms of behavior are generally beneficial and conduce to good human life in a community. The value and importance of such things is inseparable from the worth of human beings, and the appreciation of one involves the appreciation of the other.

There are, then, in addition to the benefits to the recipients of benevolence and the satisfaction to the agents, other, more important benefits of benevolence. Actions fully characteristic of kindness, generosity, and compassion tend to foster mutual good will among people, creating relationships that are pleasant and useful, forestalling antagonism and animosity, and generally providing an atmosphere in which people can work out their differences and further common goals. The concern for the good of others exhibited by people who possess these virtues, moreover, is a striking affirmation of the intrinsic worth and importance of individual human beings. This affirmation tends to support the self-esteem, and thus the morale, of those who are the objects of this concern. The view itself that individual human beings have intrinsic value and importance is central to all our values, and an appreciation of this worth is necessary for understanding our morality and our way of life.

In the first section of this chapter, I distinguished forms of *primary* benevolence, which involve a direct concern for the good of others, from forms of *secondary* benevolence. The latter involves taking as one's ideal the (primarily) benevolent (that is, kind, generous, etc.) individual, and undertaking to act as he would act. The predominant motive in so acting is the desire to be good oneself—to be as much like a good person as possible.

This is different from the motive in primary benevolence, which is a concern for the good of another. I do not mean to suggest the agent has an ulterior motive in actions fully characteristic of secondary benevolence—one might simply take the benevolent person as worthy of emulation because of his goodness. Thus, someone who is only moderately concerned about the good of his fellows might resolve to be more benevolent. The actions characteristic of secondary benevolence would benefit their recipients and would foster good will. If it were clear, however, that the agent was concerned to "be good" and *not* particularly concerned about the good of the recipient, such actions would not be as apt to bolster the recipient's sense of his own worth. The possibility of the recipient's resenting his position of dependence upon the agent is greater in such cases. On the other hand, such secondary benevolence is an acknowledgment of and a tribute to the worth of primary benevolence.

Elements of secondary benevolence are often mixed with primary benevolence. We tend to admire the benevolent and strive to be like them. It is sometimes unclear to us when we do a kindness whether we care more about the recipient or about being good ourselves. When secondary benevolence occurs in a person who is clearly deficient in primary benevolence, however, the actions that exhibit the trait will tend to have some but not all of the beneficial results of acts of primary benevolence. This sort of benevolence is also *secondary* in the sense that it depends for its existence upon the conviction that primary benevolence is a virtue and is worthy of emulation. Secondary benevolence in the obvious absence of primary can be a shallow sort of thing. Consider the "telescopic philanthropy" of Mrs. Jellyby in *Bleak House*. She spent all of her energy and time on projects intended to benefit the natives of distant Borrioboola-Gha, while completely neglecting the members of her own family and ignoring their misery. Of course, secondary benevolence need not be capricious in this way. It may be, too, that one can become benevolent in the primary sense by first practicing secondary benevolence.

Virtues and Vices

The benefits of primary benevolence, however, are of great importance in human life generally. It is hard to imagine a permanent association of human beings for the purpose of living together as well as possible in which the individuals have no direct concern for each others' good and are in this sense totally indifferent to one another. At least a part of the reason why we regard forms of primary benevolence as virtues lies in the importance of the concern for others, of which these virtues are the perfection, for a human community. For a "kingdom of ends," if I may use Kant's terminology, not only does one need law based upon the worth of an individual, but the citizens of the "kingdom" must actually value one another. Otherwise, they cannot fully appreciate the point of such law. Those who do not altogether understand the purposes of requirements cannot live intelligently under them.

An *excess* of concern for the good of others that led an individual to neglect his own needs and obligations would still have some of the most important consequences of benevolence, including the affirmation of the value of persons. This account may be used to explain why such an excess is *excessive benevolence* rather than a vice that is an opposite of the virtues that are forms of benevolence. *This* excess does not thwart the functions of benevolence, and thus benevolence is not, in Aristotle's sense, a mean between too much and too little concern for others.

VI

Conclusion

The realization that other peoples and other communities have different ways and different values is apt to be disturbing. Apparently, we have a great need to regard our own ways as fundamentally sound. The confrontation with other ways of life that are incompatible in important respects with our own tends to undermine our confidence. This is often the beginning of moral philosophy when we try to allay our doubts about the way we live. If we seek support for our values by looking at how things actually are—by studying human life and human nature—what is apt to strike us is the diversity in human life. Ethical relativism seems the likely outcome of such a naturalistic approach, which will not restore one's confidence in one's own values. Those seeking such support are apt to turn their backs on naturalism.

I have tried to show that the value we place upon certain traits of character can be given a naturalistic basis. Without denying the differences that exist, I have emphasized certain similarities between human communities, human ways of life. The same kind of living organisms comprises these communities. A most striking fact about members of our species is that they live together in communities. It is their nature to live this way. The form of life always involves conventions, which make possible such things as language, knowledge, political and social institutions, commerce, arts, etc. In learning to live such a life, a human being inherits something of the past, including some of the accumulated skills and wisdom of his community. Cooperation, mutual support, and the anticipation of problems are found in every human community, so planning for the future is a prominent feature of human life. An awareness of time and a sense of history are parts of human life.

Only if individuals have certain fairly fixed traits of character can they live successfully in this way. To have a community—people sharing a way of life under the same conventions—people must have a certain commitment to the forms of behavior that constitute those conventions. To have such commitments, people must have a sense that the way of life defined by those conventions is itself valuable. The same considerations that make the way of life seem valuable to those who lead it can often be used as a basis for arguing that various things that people in a community require of one another are reasonably required. This kind of commitment to forms of behavior is common to the type of virtues I have called forms of conscientiousness.

If the form of life that is valued is social—as human life seems by nature to be—then people's attitude toward other members of their community will be of critical importance. To value community life, one must see the other members of the community as worthy partners in the enterprise—one must to some extent value other members of the community. Members of a human community will need to have for one another, then, the sort of direct concern that one has for someone or something one values. This is the germ of the account of the functions of various forms of benevolence in human life. Such traits, if prevalent in a community, can bind together the members, promoting both individual and community morale.

A third type of trait, exemplified by courage and restraint, is concerned with the efficacy of an individual's practical reason—

Conclusion

the abilities of an individual, first, to mold his feelings and desires into plans that fit with as little discord as possible with one another and with the larger community context, and second, to carry out such plans.

All of these traits perform functions that are, in one way or another, essential to human life. If such traits were lacking altogether in a group of people, they could not live together the sort of life characteristic of human beings. When these traits are developed in an individual to a noteworthy degree, they are virtues, human excellences. When such traits are so perfected that they are virtues, the traits tend to enhance human life, to make it flourish. This is not to say that a good human being invariably flourishes. Rather, the more good people there are in a community, the better life generally in the community is apt to be. The differences in conventions from community to community and from time to time in the same community do not affect these points that are firmly grounded in the nature of things.

Bibliography

Anscombe, G. E. M. "Modern Moral Philosophy." *Philosophy*, 33 (1958), 1–19.

Aristotle. *The Works of Aristotle*. Sir W. David Ross, ed. 12 vols., Oxford: Oxford University Press, 1915.

Baier, Kurt. "Moral Value and Moral Worth." *The Monist*, 54 (1970), 18–30.

Boorse, Christopher. "Wright on Functions." *Philosophical Review*, 85 (1976), 70–86.

Brandt, Richard B. "Blameworthiness and Obligation." In A. I. Melden, ed., *Essays in Moral Philosophy*. Seattle: University of Washington Press, 1958.

_____. "Traits of Character: A Conceptual Analysis." *American Philosophical Quarterly*, 7 (1970), 23–37.

Butler, Joseph. *Fifteen Sermons Preached at Rolls Chapel*. London: G. Bell, 1914.

Castañeda, Hector-Neri. "Imperatives, Decisions, and 'Oughts': A Logico-Metaphysical Investigation." In Hector-Neri Castañeda and George Nakhnikian, eds., *Morality and the Language of Conduct*. Detroit: Wayne State University Press, 1963.

Dewey, John. *Human Nature and Conduct*. New York: Holt, 1922.

Emerson, Ralph Waldo. "Gifts." In *The Complete Works of Ralph Waldo Emerson*, Vol. III. Boston and New York: Houghton, Mifflin, 1903.

163

Bibliography

Epicurus. "Letter to Menoeceus." In Cyril Bailey, ed., *Epicurus*. Oxford: Clarendon Press, 1926.

Feinberg, Joel. "Action and Responsibility." In Max Black, ed., *Philosophy in America*. Ithaca, N.Y.: Cornell University Press, 1965.

———. "Supererogation and Rules." *International Journal of Ethics*, 71 (1961), 276–288.

Foot, Philippa. "Moral Beliefs." *Proceedings of the Aristotelian Society*, 59 (1958–1959), 83–104.

Frankena, William K. "Prichard and the Ethics of Virtue." *The Monist*, 54(1970), 1–17.

Gauthier, David P. "Morality and Advantage." *Philosophical Review*, 76 (1967) 460–475.

———. *The Logic of Leviathan*. Oxford: Clarendon Press, 1969.

Geach, Peter Thomas. "Ascriptivism." *Philosophical Review*, 69 (1960), 221–225.

Gewirth, Alan. "Positive 'Ethics' and Normative 'Science.'" *Philosophical Review*, 69 (1960), 311–330.

Hardie, W. F. R. *Aristotle's Ethical Theory*. Oxford: Oxford University Press, 1968.

Hare, Richard M. *The Language of Morals*. Oxford: Oxford University Press, 1952.

Hunt, Lester. "Generosity." *American Philosophical Quarterly*, 12 (1975), 235–244.

Lyons, David. *Forms and Limits of Utilitarianism*. Oxford: Clarendon Press, 1965.

Margolis, Joseph. *Values and Conduct*. Oxford: Oxford University Press, 1971.

Mayr, Ernst. "The Emergence of Evolutionary Novelties." In Sol Tax, ed., *Evolution after Darwin*, Vol. I. Chicago: University of Chicago Press, 1960.

Murphy, Arthur E. *The Theory of Practical Reason*. LaSalle, Ill. Open Court, 1964.

Nowell-Smith, Patrick H. *Ethics*. Harmondsworth, Middlesex: Penguin Books, 1954.

Prichard, Harold A. "Does Moral Philosophy Rest on a Mistake?" In *Moral Obligation*. Oxford: Clarendon Press, 1949.

Randall, John H., Jr. *Aristotle*. New York: Columbia University Press, 1960.

Rawls, John. *A Theory of Justice*. Cambridge, Mass.: Harvard University Press, 1971.

Bibliography

――――. "Two Concepts of Rules." *Philosophical Review*, 64 (1955), 3–32.

Ryle, Gilbert. "On Forgetting the Difference between Right and Wrong." In A. I. Melden, ed., *Essays in Moral Philosophy*. Seattle: University of Washington Press, 1958.

Sabine, George H. *A History of Political Theory*. 3d ed. New York: Holt, Rinehart and Winston, 1961.

Sidgwick, Henry. *The Methods of Ethics*. 7th ed. Chicago: University of Chicago Press, 1962.

Singer, Charles. *A History of Biology*. 3d ed. London and New York: Abelard-Schuman, 1959.

Urmson, J. O. "On Grading." In Anthony Flew, ed., *Logic and Language*, 2d series. New York: Barnes & Noble, 1966–1968.

Wallace, James D. "Practical Inquiry." *Philosophical Review*, 78 (1969), 435–450.

Will, Frederick L. *Induction and Justification*. Ithaca, N.Y.: Cornell University Press, 1974.

Williams, George C. *Adaptation and Natural Selection*. Princeton, N.J.: Princeton University Press, 1966.

Wilson, Edward O. *Sociobiology: The New Synthesis*. Cambridge, Mass.: The Belknap Press of Harvard University Press, 1975.

Wittgenstein, Ludwig. *Philosophical Investigations*. G. E. M. Anscombe, trans. New York: Macmillan, 1953.

Wright, Larry. "Functions." *Philosophical Review*, 82 (1973), 139–168.

Index

167

Library of Congress Cataloging in Publication Data ·
(For library cataloging purposes only)

Wallace, James D., 1937–
    Virtues and vices.

    (Contemporary philosophy)
    Bibliography: p.
    Includes index.
    1. Ethics.   2.   Virtues.   I.   Title.   II.   Series.
BJ1012. W353   170   77-90912
ISBN 0-8014-1142-4